A PEN

GHOSTS OF MAYFLOWER

TAMERA LAWRENCE

outskirtspress
DENVER, COLORADO

The opinions expressed in this manuscript are solely the opinions of the author and do not represent the opinions or thoughts of the publisher. The author has represented and warranted full ownership and/or legal right to publish all the materials in this book.

Ghosts of Mayflower
A Pennhurst Haunting
All Rights Reserved.
Copyright © 2013 Tamera Lawrence
v2.0 r2.0

Cover Photo by Tamera Lawrence. All rights reserved - used with permission.

This book may not be reproduced, transmitted, or stored in whole or in part by any means, including graphic, electronic, or mechanical without the express written consent of the publisher except in the case of brief quotations embodied in critical articles and reviews.

Outskirts Press, Inc.
http://www.outskirtspress.com

ISBN: 978-1-4787-1805-5

Library of Congress Control Number: 2012919761

Outskirts Press and the "OP" logo are trademarks belonging to Outskirts Press, Inc.

PRINTED IN THE UNITED STATES OF AMERICA

To those who wonder.

Contents

Introduction i

Chapter 1 1
Chapter 2 7
Chapter 3 13
Chapter 4 22
Chapter 5 27
Chapter 6 39
Chapter 7 52
Chapter 8 67
Chapter 9 102
Chapter 10 108

Conclusion 113

Introduction

BEFORE YOU SEE what's left of the *Eastern Pennsylvania State Institution for the Feeble-Minded and Epileptic,* the tree line driveway leads you back into time. The way is bumpy, the road narrow and curved. Timeworn streetlamps speak of a bygone era, a past forgotten.

Pennhurst is a huge complex. The brick buildings are massive, forbidden. Grass and weeds encroach and twist over old playground equipment. Vines cling to broken windows. Concrete walkways lead to the various named buildings, over twenty-five in all. Beneath it all there is miles of underground tunnels, once used to transport patients - both dead and alive.

Pennsylvania State School and hospital was built in 1908. It was intended to keep out society's misfits, the mentally ill and epileptics. It was designed to run as a society as itself and keep away the different from the rest of humanity. Children of all ages lived in Pennhurst. Lived their entire lives there and grew to adulthood. One would wonder as to what that life consisted? What compassion did that child receive? Were they ever loved?

Pennhurst is haunting, beautiful in its own way. Its tainted history draws me in. I want to know more of the past and the present.

In the fall of 2011, I worked in the Mayflower building from September to November. It is said to be one of the most haunted buildings in Pennhurst. It has been the source of several paranormal shows.

The following is a detailed account of what I find in the Mayflower - see. Does the dead have a message for us all? Or just for me?

CHAPTER 1

Night One in the Mayflower Building, 2nd Floor

"MOMMY," A CHILD cried out.

Frozen, I blinked beneath the harsh lighting. A child? Why would a child be in the Mayflower building at the Pennhurst Haunt? And such a young child. The sound had come from above me - the third floor. Slowly, I walked to the foot of the stairs and shined my flashlight up the stairwell. Nothing. Just creepy blackness and the feeling something was watching me. My light fell on the ceiling above. Water dripped in the corner, where the exposed ceiling dipped. Paint chips hung precariously from the ceiling. My beam trailed over the window at the top. How many people had looked out that same window? Walked that same staircase?

I moved back into position at the top of the second floor staircase. I stood quietly. I know what I heard. Could another worker in the building been mimicking a kid? Perhaps a customer coming up from the first floor with a small child in tow? I waited. Minutes ticked away. When the next group of people arrived, there aren't any kids with them. And there weren't any children for the remainder of that night. My thoughts flew over possibilities. But *ghost* echoed in my mind.

◄ GHOSTS OF MAYFLOWER

It was the first night of the Pennhurst Asylum, located in Spring City, Pennsylvania. The old Pennhurst State School had closed its door in 1986 due to allegations of abuse. It had been turned into a Halloween attraction. The building had been left to rot away. Ceilings leaked, plumbing was missing and ceilings and walls were graffiti and chipped. This was the haunts second year. It was raining outside in an endless torrent. It began raining inside parts of the building. Dripping became my companion as I waited for ghost hunters to come up to the second floor. Because of the rotten weather, customers were few and far between.

I was an orderly in the 2011 Mayflower Building, new this year to the haunted attraction. My uniform was all white. White pants, white collared shirt, white shoes. I also wore a black bowtie and belt. I decided to wear my hair in a head band to give me a more orderly affect.

Customers were given flashlights and were able to explore the first and second floors of the huge building, looking for real ghosts. The Mayflower was said to be truly haunted. Mayflower employees were already warned that we would be messed with by something haunting the building. We were informed most of us wouldn't last out the season because of it. Do I believe in ghosts? To a degree I do. Perhaps Pennhurst would make me a believer.

My job was to guard the third floor stairwell from patrons who wanted to explore the rooms above me as well as just keeping an eye on everyone in my area. The third floor was closed off for the season. The stairway was barred by a plastic chain, which could be easily broken.

Earlier in the night, I had toured the third floor with three other employees. Darkness pressed against me. It was creepy. It felt like at any moment something would reach out and

CHAPTER 1 ➤

touch me. Trailing the group, my flashlight beam created large shadows. Doorways were ominous, leading into forbidden rooms. I flashed my light behind me, trying to ward off the darkness. When our group rounded the corner into the hallway, a dark shadow crossed in front of the doorway. If I would have blinked, I would've missed it. Stunned, I hurried down the staircase, not sure what I had seen. But others had seen it too. In fact, a lot of people I meet over the next few weeks will talk of dark shadows and of children, nurses. But I passed it off to maybe it had been a shadow created by our flashlights when we passed through the doorway. I'm not ready to believe in any other possibility. I'm here to work. To learn.

I worked half of the second floor of the Mayflower building, usually standing in the small stairwell because it was lit and my source of refuge. There are three staircases leading to the third floor, however, I only have one in my area. I directed people inside the second floor rooms and watched them look for ghosts. I can stand at the top of the staircase or duck inside the door opening, and still look for anyone trying to sneak up to the third floor. When I am standing inside the doorway, I am invisible to groups until they would walk in and see me.

By the time most customers reach the second floor of the building, they are usually scared. But then there are those who wanted to go up to the third floor. I could hear them talking about sneaking under the chain but then they would see me watching them from my vantage point in the dark. I received guilty smiles. I knew they were tempted to go under the chain. Over time, several try it. I'm asked about the third floor. Some begged me to look the other way. Others offered me money. I turned them all down.

The area I worked in was divided into four sections. I will call them cells. Half walls - around seven feet high divided the rooms. Graffiti was sprawled across the worn rusty surfaces. Some walls have paintings. The one closest to me revealed a bird. There are windows in the rooms, but they have heavy metal screens. Vines of yesteryears have spread their ugliness over the windows, helping block out the light. From time to time, light flashed over the building from the tower's beacon outside. It does nothing to ease my mind.

Inside the cells, there are old mattresses. They lay tightly against the walls. They are ugly. Hideous. I wouldn't even want to touch them, let alone lie down on one. They also have pillows, just as black and gross. Old radiators grace the walls. The one nearest me was dripping water. In the area closest to the hallway, an old emergency phone still hung on the wall. It was red, damp from the rain. On the doorways of the cells, names are written. Bed one. Bed two. I wondered who these names belong to and what kind of life they had led in Pennhurst? The place was dismal. Depressing. I couldn't imagine living there. My empathy grew stronger.

I'm not alone in my job. My son, Sean, was working with me on the same floor. Having Sean nearby eased my fear of anything lurking in the dark. Sean walked along with the customers as they looked for ghosts.

On the other side of the second floor, two women and another man worked as orderlies. Jenny, a young woman wearing facial piercings, guarded the other stairwell leading to the third and first floors. The other stairwell was closed off. Lori was closer to my age. She took her job seriously and I knew I could count on her. She stayed mostly in the common room. And then there was James, young and a natural comedian. James, like Sean, wandered around the building, watching the ghost seekers.

My son, Jenny and James are free to stand in any of the

CHAPTER 1

rooms, following people around to make sure no one back tracked. They made noises and banged on the walls to scare people, which worked only too well. When my son approached out of the dark, he made quite a spectacle. He's very tall, big. His face was scarred from an accident and he purposely walked like a zombie. Women looked over their shoulders at Sean, worry on their faces. They aren't sure what to make of him.

The hours slowly passed. I strained my ears to hear the child's voice again, glad when I didn't. I have a young son and couldn't imagine bringing him into the Mayflower. He would have been really freaked out and frankly, I would have been up with him all night. No thank you. I like my sleep.

Customers came up the staircase. I could tell who was really frightened by the way they clung to one another and the ones who really wanted to find a ghost. These folks would boldly enter the room, daring something to jump out at them.

I said, "Hello," and smiled.

As the evening wore down, we whistled and pretended to be frightened of one another. We deliberately banged on walls and made scratching noises. Finally, the night was over. I followed my son and the other workers to the other side of the building. I had to go through a doorway that divided the building into two sections. On the other side of the doorway, there are also two cells, a common room and a bathroom. The common room holds rubber chairs situated around an old table. They are so old it was hard to tell exactly what color they had been. I know that I will never sit on one and avoided touching them. A desk graced one corner along with a closet of some sort. The bathroom was missing the commode but the floor was wet from the continual rain. After passing through the common room, one came to a large hallway. This also had several other rooms and another bathroom, just as awful and eerie as my side of the building. In time, the art room (what we call it) seemed to have the most paranormal activity. I didn't like being in there. I could feel something around me in the room, something sinister.

"I got tapped on my shoulder," James announced to me. He was grinning from ear to ear. His love of the paranormal was evident. Tall and lanky, James was eccentric. He was dying to be a monster in the asylum part of Pennhurst but because he was new this year, he had to put his time in at the Mayflower. We all did.

I'm not sure of his claims. I had my doubts. But in the days to follow, I began to believe.

CHAPTER 2

Saturday, Day Two

WHEN MY SON and I got to work on Saturday night, we are informed we are not to scare any of the customers. That the people are on a real ghost hunt and we're only there to guide them and keep them off the third floor. We are told we are like *ghosts* - there, but not scary.

James was highly disappointed. He lives for this stuff. "Boring," he whispered to me.

My son shrugs as we made our way up to the second floor. We are both here just to work. We both could use the extra money. But it had been fun pushing everyone's buttons the night before.

Lori came over to me. She twisted her lips, rolling her eyes. "We aren't allowed to scare anyone," she complained. "It's going to be boring."

I leaned in closer to her and spoke loudly. "Tonight should be busy. Let's just have fun watching people look for ghosts. Besides, we can still talk."

She just nodded and walked away into the darkness, disappearing through the doorway leading into the other side of the building.

GHOSTS OF MAYFLOWER

"Howie, come out to play," James cried out from darkness. He was on a mission to find the elusive Howie.

Howie was rumored to haunt the Mayflower building. I'm not sure where he came from or who he was, but he was supposedly a lost soul, who owned the toys in the Mayflower. An old ball sits on the first floor and a worn fisher price airplane on the second. Both are said to be Howie's. If you touched a toy, Howie would get you. People would say the toys moved around by themselves. The ball supposedly would roll beneath the beds on the first floor.

"How does anyone know its Howie haunting this place?" I asked my son. "Of all the people who have been through here, how would they even know?"

My son just shrugged. He doesn't believe in ghosts. He wandered away into the dark, leaving me alone by the doorway. It's hot, humid. But at least the rain had stopped.

I decided to stand at the foot of the third floor staircase, knowing people will walk around the corner to look up at it. Most do, jumping when they saw me. I just smiled. I do this for a while, but can't stand the dark stairwell at the top of the steps. It's overbearing. I thought about the child yelling, "Mommy" wondering if it would happen again.

I moved back inside the doorway, keeping a close eye on people as they came up to my floor. Most looked around the corner at the third floor staircase, others wouldn't look. They are too scared.

"Where's the little girl?" a young woman asked me.

"What little girl?" I replied.

"The one someone saw last night."

"You mean the midget?"

"Midget?" she repeated, blinking. "No, a girl."

"Someone said they saw a midget," I replied, remembering

CHAPTER 2

it well. "She never said it was a girl." I smiled innocently. After they left my area, who knew what they saw when they got to Sean's side of the building. Excited they hurried off with their flashlights, wanting to find something, anything.

I started having fun with people as they entered my area. I would greet and warn them about Howie. "Don't' touch his plane. He doesn't like it."

"How can you stand there in the dark?" became the common question of the night.

"It's not easy," I replied. It was true, but I liked working there.

The next question always came hand in hand. "Did I see anything?"

"No," I replied honestly. "But I did hear a child say, Mommy."

This always excited people. Some got terrified. Others didn't believe me.

"Some of the staff has been touched," I added. "Some had their hair pulled."

When I told people about the hair pulling, they would instantly touch their head, especially girls with long hair. Some would tuck their hair into their shirts, while others yanked up their hoodies.

"You're good," one guy told me, smiling at his girlfriend's fear. He thought I was making it up. But I'm not. The hair pulling had happened to many times to be just coincidental. These people didn't know one another, yet they had all experienced the same treatment. Something in Mayflower liked hair, usually long. Even girls with pony tails or buns got fingered. I kept waiting for my turn. My hair was also long.

Sean walked around hiding in the dark. Sometimes he stood quietly in a room. People gasped when they saw him.

He followed them around, pretending to look for ghosts as well. Nervously, they would look over their shoulders at him, not sure of his intentions.

"Hey you aren't supposed to scare us," one girl said to him.

"I'm not," he replied. "I'm just walking around like you." Innocently, he smiled. But people enjoyed his teasing.

James came running up to me out of the dark. "Guess what," he exclaimed.

"What?"

"I got tapped again. I was standing on the other side, near the back rooms and it happened again. Twice." His grin widened. "I just love it. Love it."

I stared at him, shocked. "Well I hope you didn't bring it with you." I'm not sure what *it* was but I know I didn't want it touching me.

"I'm cold," he said, holding up his arm. "When it happens cold air hits me. I get goose bumps. See?"

"Well you keep telling Howie to play with you," I said, trying to see the bumps. But it was hard to see in the inky dark. "I guess he is."

This delighted James. He skipped off into the dark, crying, "Howie, come out and play with me."

Uneasily, I looked after him. I'm hot. I could have used some of that cold air. I smiled at my own musings. In the darkness, my son whistled the Freddy Kruger song, "One, two, Freddy's coming for you...."

I whistled it to and sent a prayer to heaven. "Please God protect all of us from any evil spirits." Feeling better, I returned to my post.

As the hours went by, I got into a routine of popping my head out the doorway and listening for footsteps on the

CHAPTER 2

staircase. When I heard them, I jumped back inside the door, and pressed against the half wall. I got into this routine. As people entered, I now got into scaring them with stories of Howie's airplane, located on the other side of the building. I told them about hearing, "Mommy" and about people being messed with. This mostly motivated everyone, except the truly frightened. They are the ones who clung to someone's hands and tried to walk through my area without looking into any of the cells. I loved watching the groups searching for ghosts. The men often scared their wives or girlfriends, hiding and jumping out. And then there was Sean, who did what he did so well.

During a lull in customers, I left my post and checked on Lori, who was hanging out in the common room. She saw me and grabbed my arm.

"There's something in the bathroom."

"What?" I immediately stared in that direction with my heart racing.

Lori flashed her light into the black room. There are several stalls, but a shower portion was blocked by a wall. The floor was damp. One needed to go around the shower wall to see inside.

"It was the shadow of a head," she said, nodding solemnly. "I saw it now three or four times."

"Really," I replied, stunned. Unlike James, I take Lori's words more seriously. She was around my age, a mother needing extra money. "Well I won't be going in there," I smiled and hurried back to my post putting on a false bravo. I was getting a little freaked out. The light of the stairway beckoned to me. I stood there for a while, until I felt better.

Then I started back into my routine. I hummed, whistled and greeted patrons. I always took the same actions, peeking down the staircase, listening and then jumping back against the wall. I was really enjoying myself, now getting good at telling people stories to set the mood. Then it happened. I jumped back into position, but I didn't feel a wall. I felt what seemed like a solid shoulder against my back, as if I had just backed into someone. Instantly, I froze. It felt like my husband was behind me. My shoulder felt numb, pressure against it. People were coming up from below. Instinctively, I took four quick steps to the left side just as they arrived. I was so glad to see them. I stared at where I had been standing. No one was there. A chill washed over me. Had I imagined it?

I wondered if I was going to make it through the season. It's only been two days, and I'm already freaking out. I stood under the hallway light, staring into the inky blackness. Was something standing there watching me, laughing? My imagination was getting to me.

I shined my flashlight into the darkness. Nothing.

CHAPTER 3

Sunday, Night Three

WHEN MY SON and I arrived at work on Sunday night, it was still light outside. It was nice to see the sun. Pennhurst didn't look so scary. I stared at the old courtyards, the overgrown yards. Old playground equipment was barely visible in the weeds. I was feeling better, optimistic. Tonight, we were only open until nine thirty. I think I could handle being in the Mayflower building.

Lori and I walked up to the second floor and looked around. My son was outside, talking with two orderlies, a husband and wife team who worked the front door. The second floor had muted lighting and looked worse revealed in all its glory. Once again, pity rose inside of me for the people who had once lived there. Even if the place had ever been pristine, it had to be depressing to reside there. I thought about Howie. Perhaps if he hated people he was scared, perhaps trying to protect himself. I felt pity for him and all the others in his predicament. I won't ever know their true stories.

I explored the other side of the building, where James and Jenny worked the floor. This area had extra rooms - a bathroom and two back rooms divided into four cells that were too wet to be explored the first couple of nights. But the floors were now dry.

"That's where Howie's plane is," Lori told me, nodding solemnly.

I walked into the last cell. I finally saw it. Howie's plane. Slowly, I moved towards it and stared. It looked like the fisher price plane I had as a child. It was blue and white but minus the plastic people. It looked old and dirty from sitting on the floor. I didn't like being around it. It felt oppressive, dark. I now know why I preferred the other end of the building. Whatever was in the Mayflower seemed to be in that room. I hurried out, glad for the fading light.

Figure 1. Playground equipment in the court yard

As I got ready for the night, James approached me and Sean.

"Can I switch places with you?" James begged Sean. "Where I stand is so boring."

CHAPTER 3

James had claimed he had been tapped on the shoulder several times where he normally stood. I met Sean's eyes, wanting him to work the floor nearest me.

"Okay. I'll switch with you," Sean said, shrugging.

A wide smile crossed James's face. He clapped his hands like a small child. He had gotten his way and now was hanging out with me.

It's six thirty. Pennhurst was open. The music from the asylum resounded. Over and over the eerie tune continued – If one could call it a tune. It was more like an invitation for all ghosts to come out to play. Customers lined up outside. James watched them out the window.

"Looks like we should be getting a group soon," he announced, walking over to me. He leaned against the wall, smiling.

"Good," I replied. I liked being busy. I liked talking to the people when they came to the second floor. I listened to their stories and saw their excitement. I also liked their company in the dark.

People began arriving. James skipped off to walk around in the dark, enjoying scaring the customers when they flashed their lights across his ghostly form. Tonight, he stayed very quiet in cell one. I knew he was there, but people thought I was alone. I let them think it.

We are supposed to be quiet ghosts. In our snowy uniforms, we stand out in the dark. James was good at just hiding quietly until someone walked around the wall and saw his ghastly form. He wore a pair of comical black glasses, which made him look buggy eyed. His excitement only grew when he got shrieks and guests ran past him. After people passed our area, he would run out, laughing.

"I want to go to the third floor," James said, staring at the ceiling. "By myself. But I don't think I have the nerve."

◄ GHOSTS OF MAYFLOWER

"If you go up there and start screaming," I warned. "I'm not coming to get you."

Another group of people came. I was surprised to see a few brave kids. I smiled and greeted them, refraining from warning of anything scary. Pennhurst was scary enough without my dramatic stories.

After several rounds of guest, James came out of cell one. "Something just tickled my head." He touched his hair, running his hand around. "Just like this." He put his hand on my head and wiggled his fingers.

"Well it better not touch me," I warned, forcing a false bravo.

James was eccentric. But he can get to me. A short time later, he cried out. "There's a face looking through the window."

I looked at the door. There was an old window with a black smear across it. It often looked like a mask so I don't look at it much.

"You're imagining things," I told James, hoping like heck he was. "That always looks like a face."

"No. It was behind it," James's insisted. He shivered, feeling his arms. He looked scared. He stared through the window, eyes widening. Then he screamed, "Oh my God! A shadow just went passed the door. It's hiding in the corner."

I stopped and followed his gaping stare. We both froze, breathing heavily. Then I shrugged and walked over to the door and peeped around the corner. Nothing but the cracked wall. I backed against the half wall. "There's nothing there," I said.

"I saw it," he insisted. "It moved very quickly, passing the door." He continued to stare through his funny glasses, worry on his brow. "I know what I saw."

"How old are you," I asked, staring at his eyes, which have been enhanced by black eyeliner.

CHAPTER 3

"How old do I look?" James asked. His fear was replaced by a huge grin. My suspicions that he was messing with me grew.

"Twenty or twenty-one," I answered.

"How did you know that?"

"Because I have a twenty year old and you act just like some of his friends."

James was pleased. "Really. You have a twenty year old?"

"Yes."

James rolled his eyes to the ceiling. "I still want to go up there. I want something fun to happen to me. I want a ghost to push me over or something. Not down the stairs or anything, but just give me a good shove."

I held my laughter. James was too much. But he was very entertaining to watch.

"Go for it." I followed him to the bottom of the third floor staircase. Longingly, he looked up the staircase into the blackness.

"I might," he said. "I'm thinking about it."

Voices erupted from below. James was off and running to hide in the dark.

A mother and children came up.

"Hello," I greeted.

"Hello," they responded.

"Aren't you brave," I told the boys. Worry was etched on their features as they held close to their mother. But my words did nothing to ease their anxiety.

In between customers, I walked down to see Lori. She rushed over to see me, passing the old chairs in the common room. It was darker in this area. I didn't know how she could stand it.

"I saw it again," she exclaimed, grabbing my arm. "The man in the shower."

"Really." A chill washed over me. I could see the bathroom where I stood, but it was inky black. I realized in that moment, that I have always avoided the bathroom. Call it instinct or whatever, but I could feel an ominous presence near the area.

"And someone thought they saw something in the closet," Lori said.

The closet was a narrow chamber, not attached to the wall. It could be moved around. Nothing was in it. Usually, the door hung partially open.

"And you're still here?" I smiled at her, trying to be brave.

I'm impressed by her stamina. Lori must be a saint.

I walked back to my area. My earlier optimism fades into uneasiness. The place was getting to me. My son raced to catch up with me.

"How's it going?" I asked.

"Okay," he replied. "People are really getting freaked out in the back rooms. A kid and then a man both say they saw a shadow in the art room. They both went running out."

"What about you?" I stared at him in the murky dark. He doesn't even use a flashlight and wanders around as freely as the ghosts seem to do.

"Nothing happens to me," he said. "Everyone else around me is having things happen to them, but nothing to me."

"That's because you have a praying mother," I said, to his rolling eyes. "I pray for protection when we come in here."

He walked away into the darkness as I went to greet more customers. This time I have more information for people who asked me for it. Many wanted to know what I had seen and heard. I'm only too happy to oblige them.

"Hello," I greeted. "Tonight's activity seems to be mostly in the bathroom and around Howie's plane. Howie doesn't

CHAPTER 3

like his plane touched." I sounded like I was offering a dinner special.

My tales ignited people into a fever as they rushed off to the bathroom. I watched them, laughing. I repeated this to every group that came up.

"A man's been seen in the shower," I told a group of people.

"A man," an elderly guy said. "Why couldn't it be a woman?"

One boisterous group arrived with five large men. After hearing my claims, one young man announced he was going into the bathroom alone and was turning off his flashlight.

The other men snickered and laughed at him, rushing down to see him do it.

"Watch my spot for me," I told James and followed them. This was the bathroom that Lori kept seeing the head. Knowing that, I was a bit worried and yet wanted to know if anything would happen to the man. The customer entered the bathroom but then so did the other men. They all shut off their flashlights and waited. A high pitched scream erupted and the group came rushing out, laughing.

"Nothing happened," the younger man said, seeing me. He was incredibly disappointed. Perhaps so was I.

"You have to be quiet," I replied as an explanation. "Howie likes it to be quiet."

Another group passed by me with their flashlights. One man paused and stared my way.

"Anything happen to you?" he asked me.

"Not really," I said, not sure if anything really had. "I heard a child call out, 'Mommy.'"

"I know exactly what you're talking about," he said. "I work for Pennhurst doing maintenance around here. I work a lot in this building. I hear children's voices all the time."

GHOSTS OF MAYFLOWER

This information wrapped itself around my mind – teasing me with who the children could be.

As the night winded down, the last couple finally came through. The man was self-assured, the woman, clingy. They passed through my area without saying much to me. The woman screamed somewhere off in the distance. Since they are the last customers, I walked to other side of the building. My son was standing in the larger hallway along with the other orderlies.

"A woman had just said something pulled her hair," Sean told me. "She ran screaming out of here."

Spooked, I stayed close with the others, who quickly went over the night events. Everyone had something to say. The lights overhead suddenly lit the hallway. The building looked normal, depressing and just as bleak. I walked over to Lori and touched her shoulder.

"Well we made it through our first weekend," I said. But I wondered about the weekends to come. It seemed the paranormal activity had increased over the three day span. The disruption of ghost hunters was waking something up. Something that didn't want to be disturbed.

What would next weekend hold and would I have the nerve to face it again?

━━━━ ✦ ━━━━

Over the course of the next week, Pennhurst stayed close in my mind. I lay in bed at night and thought about what I knew of the ghostly encounters. So many people had the same experiences. Complete strangers. Yet I was witnessing the same paranormal activity over and over again. Pennhurst began entering my dreams. Sometimes the dreams were scary. Part of me wanted to just walk away from it all. I loved the fall

CHAPTER 3

season and I was spending most of it in a dark, creepy building. But I couldn't. Pennhurst was drawing me in. I began keeping a record of my experiences and was writing everything down nightly as it occurred. I wanted to finish what I had started. And if I left Pennhurst, my book would have no ending.

I decided to do some research and began digging around about Pennhurst. I went on line and read everything I could find on the subject. I wanted to be able to answer some of the questions people asked me about the Mayflower. I watched *Suffer the Children*. This documentary, filmed in 1964, revealed the shocking conditions of Pennhurst. The buildings were over-crowded and under staffed. Pennsylvania had denied the residents of Pennhurst the most basic American freedoms that we all know and love. I was shocked by what I saw and witnessed. I followed my research by watching Ghost Adventures and Ghost Hunters. I'm creeped out with what they saw and heard in Mayflower. There was a recording of a girl saying her name was Mary Mo. I thought about Mary. Was she really a girl or was she something else?

I thought about the few times I had been at Pennhurst as a child. My mother's brother had worked there and I remembered hearing some of his stories. Now they lingered in my thoughts. My mother had once driven a van of Pennhurst kids to Philadelphia on a day trip. Her accounting of the event was less than pleasant. Her sympathy was with the kids yet her words of complaint fell on deaf ears.

I thought about these kids. Where were they today? Were they still alive? I could only hope they were in a better place.

CHAPTER 4

September 30, 2011

THE AIR WAS cooler as we arrived at Pennhurst. All the orderlies seemed happy to be back. I had mixed emotions but mentally prepared myself for the coming night. Several employees were mopping water in some of the rooms, which were flooded due to the recent rain. I took my position by the doorway, standing between the third floor stairwell and the entrance to the second floor. I was hoping it would be a busy night and for the most part it was.

James worked with me again. Tonight, he was a bit quiet, not his usual happy go lucky self. I finally asked him, "What's the matter?"

James told me he has something on his mind, but doesn't elaborate. My efforts to lighten his mood went nowhere.

The building smelled musty. Even though it's cold outside, it was still warm and humid on the second floor. I walked over to one of the windows in cell two and stared out at the gathering groups of people. Taking my flashlight, I put it under my chin, staring out. People in line screamed and pointed towards me. I laughed.

The window was misty from the humidity. I drew a happy

CHAPTER 4

face. Beneath it someone else had already written 'help' only backwards facing the outside.

It's not long before Lori came running up to me.

"Guess what?" Lori's gaze was bright. "I was in the back office room and I was walking out. Something slammed into the back of my leg." She lifted her leg and pointed. "That's where it hit me."

"And you're still in the building," I said, wondering. Until now, the ghostly activity had seemed playful, childlike. Could whatever lurked in the building harm us?

People arrived in much larger groups. They were all eager to find something, anything. But I know that it's too noisy, too many bodies. Again, I'm asked what I saw or heard. I began telling guests of the happenings from the previous weekend and what had just happened to Lori. It was still early in the night to see what I could add to the mix.

James wandered around, looking a little lost. After about a half hour of this, he began to enjoy being there and stood quietly in different cells to frighten people.

From time to time, we heard noises above us from the third floor. Scraping sounds, thumps. I began wondering if the ghosts were hiding upstairs, perhaps because of the crowds.

As the night progressed, I met people claiming to be psychics. Determination marks their features as they wandered off alone without the benefit of a flashlight.

Sean came down to see me, telling me Jenny had seen a boy. Jenny and James are alike in the efforts to tease Howie. Jenny worked the larger hallway, near one of the staircases and usually handled the flashlights.

"A real boy?" I asked.

"No. A ghost?"

"Watch my spot." I hurried off to find Jenny. I'm still not

completely convinced the Mayflower was haunted. I guess I'm hoping everyone was wrong and that it was just my imagination. So I would investigate any assertions and try to debunk any claims.

Jenny was standing just inside of the hallway between the light and darkness. I really didn't know her. She was usually quiet, appearing shy. She didn't look like someone who would lie about what she had seen.

"I heard you saw a ghost?" I searched her face. She was young, pretty with an eyebrow earring. Apparently, she and James were good friends and shared an apartment.

"I did," she replied. "Right over there." She pointed to the other set of stairs leading up to the third floor. Customers aren't allowed in the area and routed the other direction. A chain blocked it off.

"What did he look like?"

"He was wearing a striped shirt and looked to be around seven. He came up from the first floor, rounded the bend and continued up the staircase."

"Are you sure he wasn't real?" The question was stupid. A real boy would never go up to the third floor by himself. Grown men had trouble going up there unless they were in groups.

"He wasn't real," she said. "He just disappeared. The chain moved after he went up."

I walked back through the common room. Darkness pressed against me. It bothered me that a child would be there in the desolate building. My youngest son was seven. It hit close to home.

Later that night, Jenny told me that in the office room there was an old shirt. A striped shirt. She says it was the same shirt the boy was wearing. Upon closer inspection of the shirt, a name was written in the tag. The name matched the name written on cell two, the room nearest the area where I stand.

October 1st, 2011

For the most part, Saturday night was busy. Large groups came through the second floor of the Mayflower. I enjoyed joking with people and telling them about the boy phantom seen the night before. Most people asked me about the little girl ghost. I assured them she was there as well, but was probably hiding due to the noise. I warned everyone not to touch Howie's airplane. This excited some of the younger men, who can't wait to temp Howie. They ran off into the darkness in search of the airplane.

James had gone up to the third floor with another employee. From time to time, I would stare up at the ceiling, listening intently. Nothing. Not a peep. The men were up there awhile and I waited to see if James would start yelling. Finally, he came down, looking very worried.

"Well, how did it go," I asked James.

"I was upstairs walking down the hallway, when something jabbed me in the leg," James said. "It felt like a needle. It really hurt." He reached down and touched his leg, rubbing it. "I know what a needle feels like and it was just like, jab."

"Maybe someone thought you needed a flu shot," I replied, smiling. Once again, I wasn't sure of James's claims. Mayflower brought out his inner child. It brought out mine as well.

"It hurt," James continued in a whiny voice. "I hate needles."

"Well you said you wanted the ghost to do something more to you," I reminded him. "Now it did and now you're complaining."

GHOSTS OF MAYFLOWER

"But not a needle," James said. He rolled his eyes to the ceiling, shuddering. For the first time, I saw fear in his eyes. Real fear, not a made up version.

As the night winded down, the head security man arrived and whispered to me that Sunday night would be a *skeleton crew*. I would be working, but James and Jenny wouldn't. I had mixed feelings about being alone on my side of the building. So far James had put on quite a show, real or not. I've enjoyed his antics and his companionship. Now I would have no one.

After security had left, James played a phone recording for me. Earlier in the night, he had gone into the back room where Howie's plane was located. He has asked the ghost some questions. Questions like, "Why are you still here? Do you want me to leave? "

At several paused areas, rough breathing erupted in the air. The sound was unnerving.

"Here that?" James said, awed. "That's not me breathing. It's Howie."

"I hear it," I replied. But I wondered if he was messing with me. It was my only hope.

CHAPTER 5

Sunday, October 2nd, 2011

SUNDAY WAS COLD and rainy when Sean and I drove the back roads towards Pennhurst. We were in a hurry because I couldn't find my car keys and we were going to be late. When we pulled into Pennhurst's parking area, I found out my flashlight was missing from my bag - most likely the result of my youngest son, who liked playing with my new flashlight.

After checking in at the Administration building, we walked to the Mayflower building. Most of the orderlies were already inside. Taking a deep breath, I went inside and up the stairwell. Lori spied me and ran over.

"Oh you're here," she exclaimed. She pressed her hand against her chest, clearly relieved. "I thought I was working the floor alone. I could have never done it without you."

"It will be hard with just the three of us," I said, staring down into the shadowy hallway. This area was where Sean and Lori would work. Off this hallway, there were two sets of steps leading to the third floor, both needing to be watched. I would be working my usual spot on the other side of the building - alone. I tried not to think about being by myself.

Mitch, the orderly from first floor came up to greet me. He gave me a hand radio, which I was happy to take since it would keep me company. I asked him if he had an extra flashlight. He promptly handed me over one with a nice strong beam. Impressed, I fell in love with the flashlight which was sleek and light.

I talked with Lori for a while, asking her questions about when she was an EMT. Years earlier, Lori had worked for a local ambulance. The ambulance she worked on had been sent to Pennhurst to pick up patients that were being relocated. Now was the perfect opportunity to ask her about her experiences and what she had seen.

"Pennhurst was closing," she said. "The patients had to be taken out of here."

"To where?"

"Some were taking to nursing homes," she said. "It was really awful. One particular man had a shirt on that was so dirty it was stuck to his skin. It was that filthy. When we took him to the nursing home, they wouldn't accept him. We were told to take him to the hospital to make sure he didn't have any infectious diseases and that he needed to be thoroughly washed and checked for lice. When we got this man to the hospital, they couldn't understand why we brought him there. No one wanted him. I felt so bad for him."

"That's awful," I said, while Lori nodded. Sympathy and compassion marked her face.

"The people were in bad shape," Lori said. "They weren't being probably cared for."

Lori told me other disturbing things, things like children being left in the Quaker building with violent residents. There wasn't enough staff to protect them. This lingered in my mind for a while. The depressing images turned my thoughts to anger.

CHAPTER 5

The rooms darkened as night settled in. It was colder in the building. Fog rolled up the staircases onto the second floor like something out of a horror movie. It was coming from the tunnels below the building and was a perfect enhancement for exploring ghost seekers.

People began to arrive in larger groups. I was glad to see them, since I was pretty much alone. They were my only company. Sean and Lori worked the other side of the building. From time to time, I heard Lori loudly ordering people to move in the right direction.

It seemed people were more rowdier this week, especially the younger crowd. Teens would stroll in, pushing and shoving one another. Boys would tease the girls, hiding and jumping out. I began warning people about Mary.

"Mary likes to pull hair and tap people on the shoulder," I said. Instinctively, girls would finger their hair, while others pulled their hoods or hats over their heads. "That won't protect you." I said. After they walked away, worried and scared, I would smile and laugh wondering if anything really would happen to them. Some of the guys complain to me when nothing did.

My stories changed with the groups. I could tell who was really serious in their ghoul hunt and I kept quiet. Then there were the groups, who loved to talk to me. I had to keep the groups moving so I made it short but scary. I warned of Howie's plane. I warned about the ghostly man in the common room, who was seen lurking around the bathroom and could be seen on u-tube sitting in a chair. I told others about the boy child, his shirt and about his name still written on cell two's wall. People loved to read the list of names on the walls. Some are reverent, others excited. Some of the more serene people begged me to try and stall customers coming up from the first floor, complaining about the noisy groups. When not pressed for time, I helped some of the people out, delaying guests at the foot of the third floor staircase, urging them to look up. Some claim they saw shadows or orbs.

After telling people about the ghost named *Mary,* men would often yell out for Mary, trying to scare their wives or girlfriends. Sometimes they would say their female companions name and yell to Mary that she had a new friend who wanted to play with her. This always brought out a shriek and a denial from these women, who would be horrified by the notion

Some people would sing, "Mary had a little lamb...little lamb...little lamb..."

One group of African American women came through. They were young, pretty and dressed more for a party than for ghost exploring..

"Anything happen in here tonight," one girl asked me. She had the same look of hope and horror on her face that most people had when asking me this.

"Yes."

The other two women shrieked, holding tightly to one another.

"Like what?" the girl pressed.

"Well tonight we heard a lot of noises, bangs and shuffles." This was true. I had heard unexplained noises in the common room and had checked them out with my flashlight, never finding the source. It seemed the ghostly entities preferred quiet with little to no people.

"A man's shadow has been seen in the common room," I said. "Near the bathroom."

"Where's that?" the girl's asked.

"Just walk through that doorway into the other room," I replied. "You'll see all the chairs and the bathroom. This man

CHAPTER 5

has been seen sitting sometimes on a chair and at other times in the bathroom."

The three women walked down into the dark, clinging to one another. They peered off into the common room. Suddenly, they all scream and came running back to me.

"We're not going in there," they cried out. "There was a man standing there." They tried to pass me to get back out to the staircase.

"Sorry, but you can't back track," I said. "You have to go that way."

"No," they all cried. They hid behind me, trembling.

"I'll go with you," I said. I boldly strolled off towards the common room. The women followed me. I stopped in the doorway holding my flashlight, peering in. A large black shadow of a man rounded the wall. Quickly, I followed it, stunned by what I was witnessing. The ghost disappeared into the corner. The women halted behind me in the middle doorway, nervously awaiting my verdict.

Stumped, I stared out into the other hallway. Other people were walking by into the adjacent rooms. Through the glassless window frame, I saw and heard Lori directing the groups toward the exit. A woman walked by dressed in black.

"That's what you saw," I told the frightened women, who were still huddled together, to terrified to move. "It was that woman. She's all dressed in black."

"No it wasn't," One woman chirped up. "He was standing over by the bathroom." She flashed her light beam against the wall. "Right there. I know what I saw."

So did I, but I remained silent. The women hurried by me and toward the hallway, still shrieking over their ghostly discovery. I returned to my area, unnerved. It could have been the woman in black. I told myself this a few times until

GHOSTS OF MAYFLOWER

I almost believed it. Still, I stood directly beneath the light at the top of the staircase, once again my source of refuge. From my position, I stared into the darkened rooms, wondering if at any moment a sinister shadow would pass by or even approach me. Finally, more people came up the staircase, and I was back in business. I now told the new people about the shadow man seen by the last group.

Mayflower certainly kept my stories flowing. Everything I said was mostly the truth. I had so many tales to pick from. Whenever I could, I tried to use them all. I also wrote them down every night so I wouldn't forget each night's occurrences.

The night began to wind down. Where earlier groups consisted of eight to ten people, now the groups were two or three people. These folks are really worried about being alone in the cells. One particular group stopped in front of cell three, peering intently with their flashlights.

"Did you see that?" one girl asked the other. Two men came up behind them, all peering at the same area.

"Yeah, I see it," their response.

I walked down to them, staring into the room. "What did you see?"

"Something in the corner," the girl replied. "We all saw it."

The group wandered off into the dark, toward the common room, leaving me alone. Once again, I chickened out and went to stand by the top of the staircase beneath the light. What had they seen? My imagination went a bit wild. Maybe shadow man was now in my area.

Noises resounded above me coming from the third floor, thumps and shuffles. Once I thought I heard a child crying, another time music. This place was getting to me. And yet, nothing had really happened to me. I haven't been hurt, just spooked.

CHAPTER 5

Two men walked up the staircase. I went inside the doorway, standing in the dark. I liked when people walked into the room, not expecting to see me standing against the half wall. The men came into the room, looking to be in their late twenties. The blond one looks around cautiously, his hands trembling.

"How can you stand there in the dark?" he asked me.

"I keep asking myself that," I said, realizing I had questioned myself many times. "I guess I'm used to it."

He shivered, looking over his shoulder at his heavier friend. Then he stared at me. "Anything happen on this floor?"

"All the time," I said truthfully. I told him about the man in the other room. The ghost seekers are eager to hear more, so I told them about the little boy in the striped shirt.

"That's not good," the heavier man said, his blond friend nodding. "Children are innocent. When they die, they pass onto a better place. It's most likely a demon pretending to be a child."

I registered this. Unease entered the pit of my stomach. I have heard this before. I think I liked believing in children ghost more than demon kids. It made it easier to work in Mayflower. I have sympathy for the forgotten children of Pennhurst. I mourned for their innocence, angry at the system and any parents that willing left their children in such a place. But I know that some of the parents didn't have a choice. Often kids had been court ordered into Pennhurst. When I had researched Pennhurst, I had read some of the court transcripts.

The men walked off and entered cell one, which was just across where I stood. All of a sudden both men came rushing out, standing in front of me. The blond one was rubbing his neck. "Something just jabbed me with something..." His face was puzzled as he sought the perfect wording.

My breath caught waiting for his dreadful verdict.

"It felt like…" he paused. "It felt like someone jabbed a needle into my neck."

My blood ran cold. First James's version of the shot, now this mans.

"Someone else said the same thing, "I said, swallowing hard. Instantly, I said a prayer in my head. "Please God keep me safe in this building."

The dark haired man rolled up his sleeve, showing me a tattoo on his arm. "This is a protective symbol," he says. "Things like this always mess with me. This protects me."

"You're better off asking God for protection," I said and was met with his reproachful eyes. I realized that so far God hadn't failed me in Mayflower. At least I hadn't gotten the dreadful shot and for the most part was left alone. It was an eerie thought that perhaps the ghosts had accepted my presence.

The men wandered off into cell three. If getting the needle hadn't been bad enough, the darker haired man came running out. "Something just cut me with a razor or something," he said. He moved into the hallway, beneath the light, turning his face towards me. Fright lay in his eyes as he lifted his chin. "Is there a mark?"

His skin looked ruddy. "I'm not sure," I replied. The men were so serious. They weren't messing around. They both were really scared and both stunned by their attacks. Worriedly, they wandered off into the common room and I wasn't sure what happened to them after that. But it was unnerving knowing a razor welding, needle giving entity was hanging around with me.

The last group to arrive was a woman with her two sons. The boys looked young, maybe fifteen and seventeen.

"I work here," the woman said. "My name is Susan. I work

CHAPTER 5

in the Administration building. I see you when you pass my area every night."

"It's nice to meet you," I replied. She looks to be about my age. I instantly liked her.

She introduced her sons and smiled. "I have the night off, so I thought I'd show my kids the Mayflower building."

The trio looked around. Sean showed up and informed me it was nine-thirty. No more groups would be coming through. I was so happy. I made it through another weekend with my sanity still intact.

Sean returned to his area, taking the woman and sons with him, leaving me alone. Quickly, I gathered my stuff, glad to be leaving. I especially avoided cell one and three. I walked into the common room, pretending to be braver than I really was. I flashed my light around the room. No shadow man. I hurried through into the next hallway.

Sean, Lori and the Susan and her sons were huddled together in the hallway, talking.

"Guess what happened to her," Sean said, staring at Susan. "Something touched her stomach."

"Really," I said.

"Just like this." Susan walked over to me and tickled my stomach. It reminded me of the tickle James had given me on my head, once again compliments of a playful ghost.

That's when I noticed her son rubbing his neck, knowing the signs.

"And then something jabbed me with something," Susan's son said, pausing as if deciding on what it was. "It felt like.... like a needle."

"That's the third time I heard that," I said. My belief that whatever in the building was harmless was quickly turning to alarm. People were being attacked.

"What room were you in?"

They all look behind me at the art room. "In there."

"That's where people are always touched," Sean said. "The art room. They have their hair pulled or are touched, especially the women. It must be a man's spirit since it always seems to happen to women."

"People are also seeing shadows and odd lights in the room," Lori added.

I absorbed the information, already knowing some of it. I have never liked the art room, never had. The few times I had been in the room, I felt heaviness around me. The room's windows faced the dreaded Quaker building. I decided to avoid the room at all cost.

"The last men through here also claimed that something said *'get out'* close to his ear," Sean said. "Both went running out."

I realized it was the same men who had just left my area, one struck by a needle, the other's supposedly scratched. It seemed that people were being selected at random. Could something about certain people draw the attention of the ghosts? What did I really know about some of the customers or what they did in their private lives?

Susan shook her head. "I worked in the tunnels last year," she said. "A lot of weird things happened down there as well. I didn't like being down there."

"I wouldn't either," I replied. I had the feeling something was listening to us. I was ever aware of the darkness behind my back. I worried that at any moment, I would be attacked by an invisible needle or have my face scratched. My skin tingled thinking about it.

"My aunt used to work here," Susan said. "She was telling me how they would line the kids up along the wall and just

CHAPTER 5

spray them with a hose to bathe them. She said there weren't enough people to wash the kids, so that is what they did."

The scene etched in my mind. Once again, I got angry thinking about it, wishing I could have done something to stop it. Yet in reality, Pennhurst had been around long before my birth. Pennhurst had a long history. Some of the staff that worked at Pennhurst had been good people. They had tried their best and had cared about the patients and residents. But there just wasn't enough help or money. The Philadelphia zoo animals had more money allotted to them for taking care of the animals than to feed and care for the children of Pennhurst.

Susan's sons walked into the common room, tempting something to touch them. Finally, they came out, the younger one rubbing his arm. "Something grabbed my arm," he said.

Okay. Enough was enough. I needed to get out of there. We all walked down the staircase to the front door. I was drained and tired. I was sick of ghosts and of Pennhurst. I was thoroughly freaked out. It didn't make it better when I got to the first floor and saw a pretty orderly standing there. She worked on the first floor.

"How did it go tonight?" I asked her. "Where do you stand?"

"It went okay," she replied. "I stand at the bottom of the staircase where you work. I can sometimes here you talking to people, singing or whistling."

"I do that a lot," I said, laughing. "To keep myself company." Or most likely to keep myself from hearing children calling out to me.

"I know what you mean," she replied. "I'm by myself too."

We shared a knowing smile. "It was really creepy tonight," I confessed. "A lot of weird stuff happened."

"Things always happen on that floor," she said. "I went

GHOSTS OF MAYFLOWER

through there with a psychic a week or so ago. She said there was an angry nurse on the second floor."

"Well apparently, she is still giving people shots," I said, laughing nervously. "Three people were attacked by her."

As I left for the evening, I was cold, numb. I had a good case of the heevey jeebies. We checked out in the Administration building, nodding goodbyes to others. Later, I lay awake in my bed. Pennhurst was heavy in my mind. I was truly shaken, not sure of where my dreams would lead me. I was almost afraid to find out. I have a history of dreaming things before they happen – ever since I had been a child. Pennhurst was wrapped up in my mind for anything good to occur.

As I drifted off to sleep, a little blonde haired girl had popped into my dreams. She wore a white flowing dress. Her eyes were large and blue. She looked really sad. She was standing knee deep in what appeared to be weeds.

"Mary" I thought, slipping away.

I hadn't expected her to be so pretty.

CHAPTER 6

October 7, 8, 9 Mayflower Building

FRIDAY NIGHT WAS crazy. The crowds grew, eagerly awaiting the newest attractions that Pennhurst had to offer. We couldn't help but get excited ourselves in the Mayflower Building. It was the people that made working on the second floor fun for me. I enjoyed seeing the different individuals come through, every ethnic group. Varying age groups arrived, along with more children. When kids arrived on my floor, despite their eager faces, I avoided talking about the ghostly mayhem in the building, fearing the nightmares they might suffer because of it.

The groups that came through were rowdy, eager to ghost hunt. I doubted much paranormal activity would happen due to the mass. Once again, there were just three of us working the second floor. It was hard to keep an eye on everyone and the third floor stairwell. Some of the cells in my area were chained off, but people would lean into the chains and they would break. People would go into the rooms and I'd have to chase them out and re-chain the doorways. These areas were roped off due to electrical cords. People didn't seem to realize or care that they could trip over them in the dark.

GHOSTS OF MAYFLOWER

Another problem I had was people trying to sneak up to the third floor. This was usually teen boys who didn't care if they were caught, wanting to explore the darkness. I was quick to stop their advances, keeping it on friendly terms.

James and Jenny weren't working with us. Apparently, James had found a new position in the tunnels. I was happy for him since that was where he really wanted to be. I wasn't sure what had happened to Jenny. Later, I had learned Jenny had quit. And so did the pretty brunet girl from the first floor. The staff in the Mayflower had been permanently reduced for the season. I missed James's antics and bright smile. It was also unnerving to be in my half of the building by myself. In between customers coming up the staircase, I was alone. Sounds from cell one kept me alert. It was hard to know what the noise was or exactly where it was located. I couldn't distinguish it or debunk it.

I was stunned when my son came in to me and told me I was asked to take the Pennhurst car and drive home a guest. With some shifting around, someone took over my spot and I was off to the ticket area where I was given the keys. The woman, I was told, was a former resident of Pennhurst. I was eager to meet her.

Martha was an elderly lady with an infectious laugh. I liked her immediately. She was thrilled to take a ride in the Pennhurst mobile. I was a bit nervous driving the car through the thick crowds (since it had been sitting in the ticket area). But soon we were off and soon turned onto Route 724 heading towards Royersford.

Martha told me how she had walked to Pennhurst earlier in the evening. She described how parts of the entrance to Pennhurst had once been lined with rose bushes. She told of the manicured lawns.

CHAPTER 6

"So was it as bad as everyone says?" I asked.

"Not for me," she replied. "People over exaggerate."

"How old were you when you lived there?"

"I was taken to Pennhurst when I was eight," Martha replied. "I lived there until I was twenty-four."

"That's a long time," I replied. I couldn't imagine what it would have been like to leave my family. "So you liked living at Pennhurst?"

"Yes. I lived with a bunch of other girls in one of the cottages," Martha replied. "Yes, there were rules. But we needed rules. Some of the girls would bang their heads. I did too. Sometimes, I bit myself. When some of the girl's parents came in to visit and saw bruises, they would accuse the staff of abuse. But I knew that the girl's did it to themselves. I was always honest with my parents and told them what I did."

The cottages separated the boys from the girls. They were intended for residents who required minimal supervision and were more self-sufficient.

I wasn't sure what to make of what Martha said. I was glad she had a good childhood. She seemed sure of what she was saying, leaving me with more questions than answers.

"Where do you live now?" I asked.

"I have an apartment by myself," Martha replied. Pride filled her voice. "I take care of myself."

"That's wonderful," I replied, smiling.

After I dropped Martha off, I returned to Pennhurst driving through Spring City. A few people waved to me recognizing the Pennhurst car. It took some maneuvering to get down the long roadway and then back in front of the ticket booth. The place was busier than ever. People were everywhere.

I resumed my usual position on the second floor landing by the staircase. When making my rounds inside my area, I noticed a group of young people by the third floor staircase. They were staring up as if mesmerized. They were very quiet, to quiet. One young man saw me and motioned me over.

"Hear it?" Excitement and fear twisted in his voice.

I stood beside them. Squeak. Squeak. Squeak. I tried not to show my surprise. Someone other than me was hearing the noises upstairs. Then came a shuffling noise as if someone was dragging themselves across the floor. It was eerie, surreal.

"We keep hearing it," the young man said, nodding solemnly. "Is there anyone up there?"

"No," I replied. I clearly heard the noises. My mind filled with all kinds of lurid images of what was happening in the above hallways. It was just too easy to image some kind of ghoul crawling around, messing with us. But then again, in my absence maybe someone had snuck up the staircase. I became concerned. "Don't anyone go up there. I'll be right back."

I rushed across the floor and spied Sean in the larger hallway and motioned to him. "Is there anyone up on the third floor?"

"No," he replied. "No one."

"I'm hearing noises up there," I said. "I think someone might have snuck up there. I'm not the only one hearing it."

"Okay. I'll check it out." Sean left me, walked to the middle staircase and went up to the third floor. This staircase was narrow and led to all three floors and the basement. It had a large black metal grate that went from the third floor all the way down into the basement. If you tilted your head, you could look through the groves. It was quite a drop off and very black at the bottom. Apparently, the metal sheeting was in place to keep the past residents of Mayflower from jumping over the staircase and falling to their deaths. This staircase was used most nights to exit folks to the first floor and then out into the back parking lot. This stairway also had the third floor steps chained off.

CHAPTER 6

I hurried across the Mayflower building, back to my position. I waved to Lori as I went by. The people by the stairs were still waiting for me. I breathed a sigh of relief. None of them had snuck under the chain. I thanked them.

"Someone is checking it out," I said, moving to the foot of the staircase. I stared up into the blackness. Time ticked away. Suddenly, Sean appeared in the dark stairwell, walking down towards us.

"Where is your flashlight?" I asked him.

"I didn't take one," he replied, climbing over the chain. "I thought that I'd catch someone walking around with a flashlight and didn't think I needed it."

"You mean you walked around up there in total darkness?" My jaw dropped. I couldn't believe what he was saying. I couldn't even begin to image what it would be like to be on the third floor, alone and without a light.

Figure 2. Me in front of the half wall

"Yes," he replied. "It was so dark up there I couldn't see my hand in front of my face."

"James would have been impressed," I said. I know I was. But inside I could envision Sean walking through the hallways with that thing dragging itself around behind him. My imagination was getting the best of me. I was surprised by his stamina.

・)・)・)・

The night continued. The crowds seemed never ending. I told my stories of Howie, the nurse and the little girl. I told of the shadow man in the common room and about the wheel chair squeaking around upstairs. People were truly fascinated over what I alleged. Some girls were so scared; tears would form in their eyes. I quickly backtracked and try to ease their fears. I told them that only people who want to be messed with are messed with. This seems to work, appeasing some, but not all. As a last resort, I would offer to escort any weepers to the other side of the building. But usually this wasn't necessary. Most girls would put on a false bravo and moved off into the darkness.

I was surprised by the amount of children coming through Mayflower with their parents. The youngest child so far looked to be around four. This funny little boy jumped into every cell, making a loud "High ya!" His hands would fling outward as he did comical karate position as if he was going to chop any spirits in half. I couldn't help but smile.

"I can see he's really scared," I said to his mother.

"He's protecting me," she replied, laughing.

Other children came in. Young girls would bravely face the dark with their mothers. I couldn't help but wonder if the elusive Mary wanted to be like them - alive.

CHAPTER 6

People began using their cell phones to see. When a group first entered the building, they were only allotted one flashlight. This created a problem when the group got split, which it usually did. I often helped guests along, shining my own light around so they could see. I pointed out areas of interest and would refer to the names still written on the sides of the cell walls. I was asked a lot of questions about Pennhurst. I was glad I had read up on some facts so that I could truthfully answer them. Most people wanted to know if the mattresses on the beds were really from Pennhurst or if it the building was staged for the haunt.

"Everything you see is original to the buildings," I said, repeating this over and over throughout the night. I had to wonder why people asked me these questions. Where did these people think the props could have come from? What store could possibly sell such repulsive mattresses? And even if such a store existed, how could it replicate the age and damage?

༄༄༄

Saturday night was a lot like Friday, except the paranormal activity seemed to simmer. Like the waves of the ocean it seemed to reach up in peaks, cresting and then falling. It rippled in the air. Right away, a woman showed me her arm, claiming she had been grabbed by something. Others talked about their hair being fingered. Still others claimed they felt ill, mostly nauseous or light headed. Once again, it seemed cell one had the most activity.

I avoided going into cell one, but would tell people to check it out to see if they had any reactions. This tested my theory that something was really in there. I would often stand in the cell's doorway to watch the groups. People talked of cold air surrounding them. Others walked into cell one with their ghost detectors. Some groups exclaimed over their crazy readings. A woman dressed in black went inside cell one with her two friends. They went into one of the corners. Suddenly the woman in black came rushing out towards me, trying to back track down the staircase.

"You can't go down that way," I said to her frightened face. "You have to go all the way through the building and down the other staircase."

She turned around, exclaiming, "I have to get out of here. Now."

The young woman's friends came rushing out of cell one, worry in their eyes. "What's wrong?"

"I got to get out of here," the jittery woman exclaimed. She avoided their anxious faces, rushing past them towards the common room,

"What did you see," her friends asked her, rushing behind her and through the middle doorway.

"I don't want to talk about it," the woman replied over her shoulder. She disappeared through the doorway as if Satan himself was after her.

So I had been right. Not that I wanted to be. Something was in cell one. It was proving to be true. When alone, I heard noises in the cell and felt eyes watching me. In between customers, I would step back into the hallway, into the light. *This might be my last night,* I thought. My nerves were stretched to their breaking point.

Towards the end of Saturday night, I heard a familiar voice from down below, on the first floor. It was my son, Josh touring the Mayflower for the first time. He had known I worked there, but he didn't know where I was standing or what floor I was on. A chirpy voice spoke out to him – his pretty girlfriend, Erin.

CHAPTER 6

Since it was late and the crowds subsided, I ducked into cell two and waited in the corner for them to come upstairs.

"Where's your mother?" Erin says when entering my area.

"I don't know," my son replied. "She's got to be here somewhere."

I gently tapped the half wall.

"Did you hear that?" Erin said. Fear laced her voice.

I did it again and then scraped my flashlight over the wall, creating a creepy noise.

"What is that?" the couple said over and over again. I heard them searching the cells, worried about them being in cell one. But then my son came into cell two with his back towards me. I put my hands out in front of me and stepped out of the corner, yelling, "boo."

My son jumped and turned towards me. "I didn't see you. You scared the heck out of me."

I laughed, enjoying the moment as Erin joined us. My son told me about the tunnels and how scary it had been. "Going first through the tunnels really gets you in the mood to come in here," he said. "You're already scared from the other attractions so when you come in Mayflower, everything stands out."

"What are we supposed to be doing in here?" Erin asked me.

"You're supposed to be looking for real ghosts?"

"Really," she replied. Excitement filled her features. "Is it really haunted?"

Slowly, I nodded. "I think it is. To many weird things have happened."

After a few more minutes of talking to the couple, they moved out of my area. Once again, I was alone. Cell one bothered me. Again, I felt eyes watching me. I walked over to the entrance and flashed my light inside the small chamber. I shinned it along the corner wall where I believed something was lurking. Suddenly my flashlight dimed, flickered, went out, then came back on.

"Don't mess with me," I told the invisible thing.

I quickly moved back into the stairwell. A short time later, we were all released from our positions in the building, and I was on our way home.

Sunday night was quieter. Sunday crowds weren't drinking and partying like the Saturday's night's crowds. It appeared most people were in Mayflower to explore the building, enjoying the historical aspect, then for any spirit activity. I heard a lot of speculation, a lot of rumors and was asked a lot of questions. People talked about living in the Spring City area and visiting the place as a teen. Most illegally. Some people would know someone who had worked at Pennhurst once upon a time. Everyone would comment over Howie's plane, assuming it was for the children living in Mayflower. But Mayflower was mostly men. The toys often had another use - adult therapy. Often my ghost tales fell along the wayside. I found myself telling what I knew about Pennhurst's history and the Mayflower building. I told about how the building had been overcrowded and was ridiculously understaffed.

The Quaker building also became a topic of conversation. People wanted to know where Quaker was located. An easy answer, since it was right next to Mayflower. A lot of what I'm told was controversial. Everyone had an opinion – both good and bad. I tried to keep an open mind and kept my personal opinions to myself, sticking to facts. I also had to keep the lines moving which wasn't always easy to do when people wanted to discuss the Mayflower with me.

CHAPTER 6

Cell one still felt dark, eerie. Once again, I avoided it. I almost felt that whatever was in the cell one was hanging around me. Perhaps it liked the attention I sent its way because whenever I told the customers that something was in the cell, they would rush inside the room, trying to hear or feel something. Once again, I'm surprised by their reactions. Various people complained they were nauseous, rushing out holding their bellies. Others talked of the cold spot in the corners, the sudden chill. Others were touched, shocked when something happened. Others left my area disappointed.

The crowd grew less in numbers as the night winded down. A group of boisterous young men entered my floor, spied me and rushed over.

"Hey, did you see anything in here?" I thought about the question. It's getting to the point that my answers could go in any direction. I have seen, heard and witnessed so much - but how to explain it in just a few words. So I told them about Mary. They liked this, immediately calling out to her.

"Mary, come out Mary. We want to play with you, Mary," they kept calling, laughing and thumping on one another.

"Be nice to Mary," I teased. "Or she might get you."

They loved this, really yelling for her, begging her to touch them.

"Are you friends with Mary?" one of the teens asked me.

"No," I replied, without really thinking about my answer. "I'm not."

The group rushed out of my area still calling out for Mary to come. Their voices resounded from the common room.

Suddenly, I'm alone.

Cell one caught my eye. A cold chill washed over me. I've have the uncanny feeling that I made Mary angry with my answer. We weren't friends and she didn't like it. Angry energy

GHOSTS OF MAYFLOWER

moved around me. My flashlight dimmed and then flickered. It brightened and then went black and then brightened again. I rushed into the hallway. From the safety of the light, I stared into the inky darkness. I turned on my flashlight. It worked fine.

"Leave me alone," I said to the darkness.

A few more people came up the staircase, but I stayed in the hallway. I was jittery. The place was getting to me again. I was having trouble dealing with it. The radio on my hip came alive. Only five more people left to go through the Mayflower. But seven came up the staircase. I waited for the next five. It grew quiet. To quiet. Where was everyone?

Silence became my companion. Not a peep anywhere.

"Anyone down there," I yelled down the staircase. No one answered. I walked down the steps, staring into what seemed a black pit of despair. Earlier in the night, a lady showed me a captured picture of a white mist hanging over one of the beds on the first floor. It appeared to have some kind of face. The first floor seemed darker than the second. I walked back upstairs.

I stood at the top of the second floor staircase, staring through the doorway at all of the cells in my area. Cell one seemed ominous. I left the refuge of the hallway and entered the floor. My flashlight worked. I intended to walk quickly passed cell one so I could exit Mayflower from the larger staircase on the other side of the building. As soon as I entered the room, my flashlight went black. Unnerved, I stepped back into the hallway, into the blessed light. I was freaked out. My faith in my prayers had fled. Fear had set its ugly sights on me.

"Sean," I called out. On any other night, he was always chasing me down so we could leave. No one answered me.

I waited for another minute. Finally, I saw a light in the distant hallway.

CHAPTER 6

"Mom," Sean yelled. "What are you doing in here? Everyone is outside."

"Come over here," I yelled to him.

"What for? Come across."

"I want your flashlight," I called back, not budging from my spot.

Finally, he walked over to my side of the building. Relieved, I went to meet him. He looked at me curiously. "What's the matter with you? Why wouldn't you come across?"

"My flashlight was acting up," I replied. Eagerly, I walked through the common room and into the other hallway, exiting down the staircase to the front of the building. Everyone was outside, waiting to be cleared. My feet hurt. I was tired. But mostly, I was worried about working in Mayflower the following week.

Would Mary make me pay for not claiming her as friend?

CHAPTER 7

OVER THE NEXT few days, I bought myself two hearty looking flashlights. I find another one at my house and then threw them all into my bag. The bag I was using was a black bag with a large pumpkin face. I kept extra water, gum and my keys in this bag, which I hid on the larger staircase, out of prying eyes. I now had four flashlights. If I wanted to, I could have a flashlight in every pocket, an arsenal for protection. I pictured myself holding a flashlight in both hands, so I could shine them in two different directions. This brought a stupid grin to my lips.

I told Sean my fears about cell one. He thinks I was being absurd.

"I mean think about it, Mom," he said. "What has really happened to you? Nothing really. Things happen to everyone else."

"You haven't had anything happen?" I frowned. It wasn't fair.

"The only thing that I saw was a chain moving by itself," he admitted. "No one was near it and it was really swinging fast."

I thought about what he had said. He was right. Nothing

CHAPTER 7

happened to me. Just around me. To other people, who seemed to be the ones wanting it to happen. I felt better about going back on Thursday. Sean was making sense.

⁂

Thursday night, I went into the Administration building to clock in. Sean was lagging behind, talking to other workers out on the walkway. The Administration building was just as creepy as the Mayflower though it had a lot more people in it – something we lacked in our building. The orderlies from Mayflower didn't have to be at Pennhurst until six, while actors needing makeup for other attractions had to be at Pennhurst at four-thirty.

From time to time, I would pass some hideous looking ghoul out on a break or see them in one of the Administration building's hallway. Men and women would walk by me with grotesque faces. Fake blood and wounds would be on others. One large man had a devil face with two impressive horns. As an orderly in Mayflower, we only wore our white uniforms. Once upon a time, I had thought it would be nice to be an actor in an exhibit, but now I found I was glad I didn't have to wear all the makeup.

As I approached the check-in area in the Administration building, a woman was sitting by the office door. She looked up at me and handed me a form.

"Could you fill this out?" She smiled at me.

"What is it?"

"We are from the Travel Channel," she replied. "We will be filming tonight and need this form filled out. Please put on the bottom what position you work in."

I took the form, read it and finally signed my name. I wrote Mayflower, 2nd floor on the bottom. Budding excitement filled me. I watched the travel channel and really like some of their shows. When I got to the Mayflower, Lori was waiting by the entrance. We went upstairs, talking.

"There are chains across all of the rooms," Lori said. "Every single one."

I wasn't that surprised. The week earlier had been rough, especially Saturday night. The crowd had been rowdy, but fun. But there was a few that had taken it too far.

After a bit of time elapsed, men from the Travel Channel came through with cameras, videoing the rooms. We leaned against the walls, watching them. They passed by us, nodding greetings. After they left, I thought that was that. But I couldn't have been more wrong.

As the evening got started, I began telling my ghost tales, especially about the angry nurse and her piercing needle. We weren't very busy, being a Thursday night. A man and wife came in, looking very serious. They were an elderly couple, both with flowing gray hair.

"My wife's clairvoyant," the man told me. His face held a reverent glow. He was proud of his wife and it showed.

"Well this is the place to be," I said, nodding. I watched them move to cell one's doorway. They stood quietly, studying the room.

"Can my wife do a reading?" the husband asked, looking hopefully at me. "Can we go into the room?"

I considered his request. Cell one interested them. I could see it in their faces. They were picking up something in the room – something that I knew was there. Last week the couple would have had their pick of rooms to explore. But now the chains were in place. We weren't busy so I said, "Okay. But only until the next group comes ups the staircase. Then you got to get out."

They both ducked under the chain. I leaned against cell

CHAPTER 7

two's wall, waiting for the sound of footsteps on the staircase. Time ticked away. The couple was so quiet that I wouldn't have known they were there.

The couple finally came out. Finally, the woman spoke. "There's something in the corner," she said. "I can feel its anger. Its fury."

Her words washed over me. I knew there was something in the corner. I always felt the thing, but to hear someone else verify it was icing on the cake - a chilly frosting.

"I didn't go near it," the woman said. "It doesn't want me in there. I stood in the middle of the room but I could feel it."

People began coming up the staircase. Heeding my words, the couple moved off, looking into the other cells. Customers passed by the husband and wife several times as they studied the other cells. I wondered if the couple was going to ask me to go into each cell, but they didn't. In time, they thanked me and moved on.

Another group of people came up to the second floor. They were eager to know all that I knew. So I told them. They lapped it up like starved dogs. I was enjoying myself. I noticed a dark haired woman watching me from the hallway. When the group moved on, she came into the room.

"Can you tell me everything you just told them," the petite woman asked, moving in front of me.

"Sure," I replied, smiling.

"In front of a camera," she said.

My smile froze. A camera?

A group of people came in from the hallway. The Travel Channel. Like a deer in the headlights, I was taken off guard. I now recognized the woman who had handed me the permission form in the Administration building.

"Okay," I said, wishing I had more notice.

GHOSTS OF MAYFLOWER

My heart leaped to my throat as I began telling them about the angry nurse and about the little girl. I was nervous, unprepared. But they just kept taping me. When they were finished, they thanked me and moved off into the common room. I spent the next half hour rehearsing what I had said in my head, trying to remember what stories I relayed and wishing I could have planned for the moment. Perhaps they would review the tape and find me lacking, not good television. I could only wonder what they would do with the footage.

A group of men came up the staircase. They had on interesting pumpkin shirts that read Haunt World. I told the first man that I liked his shirt. He said," thanks." The men stopped in front of me, asking me if I saw anything paranormal. I easily told them Mary and Howie, wishing I could have sounded so at ease in front of the earlier camera. I told the men about cell one, about it having the most paranormal activity in my area.

"Mind if we go in there," they asked me. "This is what we do."

"Sure, go ahead."

The men ducked beneath the chain. They stood in the dark cell, quietly. Customers were few and far between. It had been a great Thursday night for serious ghost hunters.

Finally, the men came out.

"Anything," I asked the group.

"Something felt like it was pressing into my shoulder," one man confessed.

"Like a needle?" I said, noting the signs.

"Well maybe like a needle, only they couldn't get through my thick shoulder."

I told him about the nurse and all of the people who had gotten the awful shot. The man smiled, obviously very happy his shoulder was impenetrable.

CHAPTER 7

The men looked around some more and then left my area. It was later that same night when I had found out that the gentleman that I had spoken with had an experience with something in the art room - that the same man got a great picture of something next to the closet. The next day, I got to see the picture firsthand from one of the other orderlies. I stared in awe. It looked like a misted figure holding the hand of the man. The mystic ghoul was large.

Sean went into the art room to see how big the entity had been. He guessed it to be around his size, six four, or five. It was unnerving to say the least. I hadn't expected any of the ghosts to be so huge.

﹌﹌﹌

Friday night was really busy. The crowds were rowdy, excitable. With most of the first and second floor chained off, the crowds moved along better. Lori was upset because she read something on face book about an orderly yelling at people the night before. She was so upset. We all assured her that she was doing a great job. But still her tears flowed.

"Do you want to try someone else's spot?" I asked her. Perhaps she wouldn't have to interact as much with the crowd. She seemed a bit forlorn, but decided to change with me. Now she would be at the top of my staircase and greet the people coming up from the first floor. After that, they would leave her area and come into mine. Now I was responsible for keeping an eye on the common room and exiting the crowd down the staircase.

This was an interesting change for me. I was in the larger hallway, standing near the art room. I didn't like the art room. It felt dark, foreboding. I also had a good view of Howie's airplane, which had been moved into one of the smaller rooms.

◄ GHOSTS OF MAYFLOWER

At first I didn't like my new spot. I didn't get to talk to the ghost seekers as much. I was more or less trying to watch everyone at once and also be polite.

But that all changed.

I could see the excitement in some of the customer's faces when they got to my side of the building. A lot of people were staring down at their cell phones, heads bent in hushed excitement. When they came around the roped areas towards me, I would approach and asked them to see their pictures. They were all happy to oblige me.

I was stunned by what people were capturing. Some of them were very impressive. One lady had misty figure over a bed downstairs. Some had pictures in the common room of shadows, orbs. Someone else had what looked to be a man sitting in one of the common room chairs. This was the second time I had seen a picture of him. One woman said something gently ran its hand down her hair on the first floor. Someone else claimed they saw the little girl. The stories went on and on.

I went home that *night* astonished by all I had seen and witnessed.

⁂

On *Saturday* night we were told by our supervisor that Pennhurst was expecting over five thousand people. By mid-evening, the parking lots were already crammed full. Pennhurst had to turn people away. There just wasn't anywhere to put the autos.

I took a peek out the windows a few times, impressed by the huge array of cars trying to move forward in the road leading to the parking area. The groups that came to the second floor were larger, more rowdy. Alcohol lingered in the air. It

CHAPTER 7

was going to be a long night. Already my feet were hurting. I would hop up and down on one foot, twist and turn my ankles. I had another helper, Nina, who sat in the back area at the end of the large hallway. This area was also divided into four cells and was the darkest rooms on my side of the building. These cells were also the hardest to watch since they were farther away from where I was standing. But Nina sat on a table between the four cells, talking to people as they passed by her. I heard her repeating my ghost stories about Mary, Howie and the man in the common room that I had shared with her.

Sean was outside, collecting flashlights. When Lori needed a break, I took over her spot, Sean in mine. I stayed in Lori's areas for about ten minutes. I stared at cell one, but for some reason it didn't seem ominous to me. I had to wonder if the thing in cell one had moved to the other side of the building with me. Even though the crowds were fierce, I still had a lull between customers. When it would quiet down, I heard thumps and shuffles on the third floor. But then I heard a new sound – the sound of a creaking wheelchair rolling along the third floor hallways. Apparently, the ghosts, for the most part, were staying hidden on the third floor. I couldn't blame them.

I didn't get to talk to the customers as much as I would have liked. I had to keep the lines moving and conversations held up the lines. People would ask me questions and I tried to keep my answers simple. I didn't elaborate so much on the ghostly mayhem because people would just stop in the line to look for the spirits. I couldn't even tell the ghost seekers where most of the paranormal activity had been happening because once again, this would hold up the line. Instead, I encouraged people to come back on a Sunday or Thursday when we weren't so busy. Over time, I saw a lot of faces returning, smiling and asking me if I remembered them.

"Yes," I would say, smiling. Perhaps a bit of a white lie.

We didn't get to leave Pennhurst until after three am. We began wishing each other good morning and ate cold pizza, compliments of Pennhurst. My toes were numb. I was chilled and so tired. But all and all, I felt pretty good. For once, I liked being in the Mayflower building and part of the Pennhurst team.

Early Sunday morning, I had taken out my camera from my Pennhurst bag to get developed at a nearby store. It was a disposable camera that I had used in Mayflower, over a period of several nights. I had been trying to capture pictures of ghosts or orbs or perhaps disprove they were even there.

This was the second roll of film that I was getting developed. The first roll I had developed the previous week. On those photos I had gotten a few pictures with orbs and squiggly lines. Some of the orbs looked like shoe strings.

I couldn't wait to get my new roll of film developed, hoping to have gotten some good shots. When I was getting ready to leave for the store, I noticed I had two remaining pictures on the camera. I decided to snap the last two pictures and use up the film. I took the first picture out on my front lawn, which had been decorated for Halloween. I then took a picture of Storm, my kid's cat on my back porch. I then got into the car and took the roll to a one hour photo, dropping it off for processing. It wasn't until a few hours later, that I actually picked up the pictures.

My daughter and I went through the photos looking for anything strange in the pictures. There were a lot of images of orbs and more wiggly lines. But then I came to

CHAPTER 7

the pictures taken earlier in the day at my house. I was stunned. On my front lawn there was a flaming bolt with what appeared to be a skull head. The other photo, which had been taken on my rear porch also revealed the same fiery streak. Of course, I tried to rationalize the pictures. *Could it have been the sun?* Well, no. The front of my house had been shaded. The sun hadn't come up from behind the house yet. And the back porch photo was always shaded until later in the day.

So maybe *it was a flaw in the film*.

Hmmm. You be the judge.

Figure 4. Strange picture in front of my house, looks like a skull head.

The rest of the photos came out just fine. But still, I held out hope for any other possibility. But the reality was that I had seen similar pictures of the fiery skull thing at Pennhurst. And you could say this fiery orb bears a resemblance to *Ghost*

GHOSTS OF MAYFLOWER

Rider without his motorcycle. I had also seen a picture that was taken at Pennhurst of the fire breather. This man entertained people waiting in line for the haunt. In one of his photos a strange skull seemed to be in the flame, looking eerily similar.

Could something from the Mayflower have followed me home? My family was skeptical, but my daughter was afraid. I told her to pray and she would feel safer. I decided that if something had followed me home, it needed to go back to Pennhurst and now. But I put it out of my mind Sunday after noon.

Sunday night I arrived at Pennhurst only to find out I was working the second floor by myself. Sean and Lori would be on the first floor. I thought I could handle it, but when I was standing alone at six-thirty in the large hallway, I was unnerved. It was quiet.

Just me and all the ghosts.

Occasionally Sean would yell up to me to make sure I was okay.

"Sure," I'd yell back down the staircase. All of the darkest rooms seemed to have eyes watching me. I whistled and then hummed. I wondered if the flaming skull head had followed me back to Pennhurst or was still wandering around my front lawn. I was hoping it wasn't hanging around inside my home. Perhaps it couldn't find its way back to Pennhurst.

I couldn't help but wear a stupid smile. It all seemed so absurd.

Soon I broke out in a song. The acoustics were great in the Mayflower. My son yelled up to me that I was weird. I didn't care. It helped me keep my sanity.

Finally, people began entering the building. Relieved, I waited for them to make their rounds and come up to the second floor. The crowd was great. The people were so much fun and so eager to find a ghost.

CHAPTER 7

"Who graffiti all over the walls?" one young girl asked me.

"I did," I said and then smiled to her shocked face.

"People vandalized the property," I confessed. "The buildings were empty for many years."

Since the crowds weren't that bad, I had gotten to spend more time talking to people and saw more of their ghostly pictures. I told them my Mayflower stories, but then there was the truly curious, who wanted to know exactly what Pennhurst had been about.

"Pennhurst was a state school and mental institution," I said. "It housed children that grew to adulthood. Children as young as four could be dropped off. Some were left off by their parents, others court appointed. Most of them lived here their whole lives. The luckier ones got to leave in 1986. Over the course of Pennhurst's life, over ten thousand people had passed through its doors."

"Where did the Pennhurst people go?" I was asked by several guests. It was a common question.

"Some went to nursing homes, others back to their families. But a lot were just left off in the streets. These were people who didn't know how to care for themselves. They were homeless. Some returned to living in Pennhurst's empty buildings. The state didn't do them any favors."

It wasn't easy to watch the whole floor. I had to make sure people weren't ducking under the chains and keep the lines moving. The two biggest incidents of the night came when a group of young people slammed shut the closet doors in the common room and began throwing around the furniture. I gave a shout of warning through the glassless window. They quickly got out of the area and headed into my hallway, back towards the darker cells. A chain popped at the end of the hallway. I left my spot and hurried in to find this same group of people hanging out in one of the back cell rooms, now minus its chain. They tried to act innocent as if the chain had broken by itself. But I knew better. I was on the verge of calling security for assistance. But then the rambunctious group hurried past me and thankfully, headed for the exit.

As people passed by me to exit, a woman told me a couple of people were in the back cell rooms drinking alcohol. I rushed to the end of the hallway. But something was odd. All of the people in line were on the left side of the rope. No one was on the right side. The line had just stopped as people frightfully stared at a chain that was swinging violently in front of one of the cell's doorways. They were all afraid to go past the cell.

"That's moving all by itself," they told me in hushed excitement.

Ignoring them, I ducked beneath the rolling chain, flashlight in hand. I swung the light around in every corner. No one was there. Everyone was quite impressed that I went into the room. They said as much.

"Aren't you scared?" someone asked.

"I thought someone was back there," I replied, climbing back under the chain. "That could be why the chain was moving."

"No one was in there," people insisted. "That's why we were all just standing here. We were all watching the chain move by itself."

I walked passed them to look into the other cells. All empty. Apparently whoever had been drinking had moved on, probably hiding their cans or bottles in coats or pockets. As I resumed my position near the exit, I looked for bulges but never did find who they were.

People were taking pictures on their cell phones. Once

CHAPTER 7

again, I was impressed by the ghastly images. Inside the exiting stairwell, a woman had captured a face peeking around the corner. This area was lit, yet the ghoul didn't seem to mind the light. Others took photos of the same spot. Some had trouble with their cameras or phones. One woman took a shot of a white blur. Another captured a misty image looking like it was taking off in flight over the staircase. Someone else captured what looked to be a child near the airplane. Another had a shot of what appeared to be the whimsy little girl hiding out in the filing room. Orbs were also everywhere. Tonight was a good night for pictures.

Another one of my son's arrived with his girlfriend. Tim is a no-nonsense, practical twenty-year old, who loved history and was a computer whiz. He didn't believe in ghosts, but did believe in God. He didn't like my claims that Pennhurst was really haunted and was determined to debunk my claims.

Another acquaintance of our family arrived. Jake and two teens arrived, stunned to see me working in Mayflower. Jake's boys were so excited about being in the Mayflower and began taking pictures on their cell phone. They ended up following Tim around. I told them where the best paranormal activity always happened and where people got the best pictures.

Tim and his girlfriend began taking pictures too. But it was Jake's boys that were getting the best shots. They had an image of a white light leaping out of the bathroom wall, another of several orbs. They got pictures of dark shadows and what looked like a face in the art room. The list goes on and on. Since it was near closing when they had arrived, my son had taken his time exploring the rooms. So had Jake and his boys.

My son wanted to see the third floor. Years earlier, he had been in the Mayflower with a couple of friends. He claimed they had closed all the doors on the third floor and then went downstairs to explore. One of Tim's friends had lost his phone on the third floor. They had all went back upstairs to look for it. When they arrived on the third floor, all the closed doors were now open. Still, having this experience didn't seem to bother Tim. He was still skeptical.

The second floor emptied of people. I had taken Tim and his girlfriend to the third floor hallway and let them walk through it. No sooner had we entered the area when a voice came out of the dark.

"Hurry up," Sean said in the dark. "They're coming."

I wasn't sure who was coming or if late customers were arriving. We hurried down the staircase. No one was around. Sean was nowhere in sight. In fact, Sean wasn't even in the building. He was out front with the other orderlies.

"Did you yell up the staircase to us," Tim asked Sean, who finally came up to the second floor.

"No. I was outside handing out flashlights."

We never knew who the voice had belonged to. I could only guess, but not say his name. But it will be awhile, maybe never till I go up to the third floor again.

CHAPTER 8

Forgotten Souls

BEFORE THE START of a new weekend at Pennhurst, I had taken a lot of pictures at my house, looking for any signs of the fiery skull head. To my relief, the photos all appeared to be normal, though my daughter claimed several had orbs in them. I told her it was dust, hoping it was. I did a lot of praying that anything that shouldn't be in my home would leave and not come back.

I had spent long hours standing the previous weekend and my feet were still a bit achy. Since I was writing about Pennhurst, I spent a few hours reading additional court reports and then watched news footage from the nineteen sixties. I absorbed as much information as possible. I also watched news reports from other countries about institutes similar to Pennhurst. Some were really brutal. The sad part was the suffering was still going on these other countries. At least Pennhurst had been closed down. These other institutes were still in operation. After watching the disturbing images , I felt depressed and was sickened by the small children stuck in metal cribs, crying for someone to hold them, to love them. Some of their spines and limbs were twisted into odd positions from lack of use. Children that were fifteen were as big as six year olds, having their growth stunted. As hard as it was to watch such things, it's important that the truth be known to create changes, to reach humanity's heartstrings.

October 20th

Thursday night was a beautiful evening with star speckled skies. But it was noticeably cooler. The wind whipped through the autumn leaves, stirring branches and creating a tantalizing effect around the Pennhurst Haunt. The over grown play yard looked strangely beautiful with its overgrown weeds twisting around the rusted playground equipment.

I stood a moment, staring at the massive buildings. I studied the various windows and doorways thinking about the people who had once walked through the doors, looked out the windows. I walked around the Mayflower building, studying the various exits. One area behind the building had changed into what appeared to be a mini lake overnight due to the excessive rain on Wednesday. The wind rippled the water. Crusted leaves swirled in the breeze, landed in the water and floated in clusters.

I noticed what looked to be news people coming up the walkway and went to stand with the other orderlies just outside the Mayflower entrance. The small news group consisted of two men and one woman. They held recording and camera equipment. One of the young men talked to Mitch, the first floor orderly and then they all went inside to walk the floors before Pennhurst opened for the evening.

I talked to Lori a few moments and then accompanied her up the staircase. It was just the two of us working the second floor for the evening. Lori would greet the people entering our

CHAPTER 8

floor and I would exit them out the main hallway and down the smallest of the staircases.

As usual, I stared down into the ominous main hallway, hating the darkened areas which denied my sight. Lori chatted away to me. She seemed immune to the eerie atmosphere. Upstairs, I heard the news group walking along the floors. After a few minutes, they came down to my area. Lori stood off to the corner as they approached me.

"Do you work this floor?" the taller man asked me.

"I do." I shared a smile with him.

The woman asked me for an interview. They wanted to know about everything I had seen or witnessed. I began telling the same stories I told most of the ghost seekers. About the nurse, the little girl and the man who haunted the common room. I showed them where most of the paranormal activity lingered and watched them take photos, hoping to get something on camera.

When we finished, they thanked me and told me they were from Cabrini College. They headed off downstairs to film arriving customers.

Lori went over to her area, while I rifled through my bag and found my drink. I took a few minutes, walking along the hallway, staring into various rooms. Outside the gray sky was fading to black. Customer began entering the Mayflower building. The night was off and running.

Thursday night's crowd held a lot of families. Children were with parents, nervously staying close to them. I spent a lot of time giving what history I knew to people eager to know more about Pennhurst. One question was routinely asked, "Who did the graffiti?"

People would comment about some of the names on the walls. One man told me one marking was that of a Mexican crime gang. I wasn't sure of his statement or if there was any truth to it.

People talked a lot about the cat picture in the main hallway. It was an image of a feline staring out of a window. It was located in the middle of the hallway, pretty high up on the wall. At first glance it looked like a painting but if you looked closer, it seemed to be a sticker or decal on the wall. But nonetheless, it was often a topic of conversation. I was questioned about it and where it had come from. I could honestly answer, I haven't a clue. But it did seem out of place in the morbid hallway.

People weren't happy about not seeing any ghosts. Nothing was happening to anyone. No photos. No hair pulling. No needles. No touches or noises.

The night seemed void of ghosts. I didn't feel anything on my floor. Call it instincts or whatever you like, but I could tell when something was around me. And it had felt like just an old building.

"Where are the ghosts?" People asked me as if it was my fault for the no show, and I could do something about it.

"I think they are on the third floor tonight," I replied. "You'll know when they're here. They will mess with you."

Customers either give me strange or hopeful looks. In the hallway, a few people called out, "Please touch me."

The lines kept moving along. Another hour passed by. I began hearing thumps and shuffles on the third floor. Something was waking up. I could sense it. Perhaps the people were drawing it. The crowd didn't notice. They were busy talking to one another or observing the rooms. I waited, feeling the change in the air around me. Something was now on my floor.

Finally, a man came by the exit.

"I saw the little girl in the back room," he told me.

CHAPTER 8

The man said it casually, without fear or regret. I wondered if he was just making it up. But I decided to use it and started livening up the hallway with my talk of the little girl. When people heard she was in the back room, they eagerly rushed to find her.

"How can you work in here," one woman asked me just before she exited down the stairwell.

"I decided to give my guardian angel a workout," I told her, smiling.

"Good answer," she replied, laughing.

Another group of young women stood around me. We had a heart to heart about Pennhurst. They were deeply moved by the resident's plights and what happened to the remaining people. So I told them what I knew and about how the last residents of Pennhurst were taken to nursing homes or were taken in by family members.

"Some of the homeless came back to Pennhurst, not knowing any other home," I said.

"That's so sad," one woman said. "But it makes sense."

"Pennsylvania didn't do anyone any favors when they closed Pennhurst the way they did," I said. "That alone was a crime in itself."

The night began winding down. The last few groups were eager to find a ghost. Once again, I told of the little girl in the back room. About fifteen people moved into the area. They were the last of my groups and stayed the longest in the back corner cells.

All was quiet. Then all of a sudden a woman and man came rushing out of the dark.

"We saw her," the man exclaimed to me. "She was near the window. We all saw her."

"You did? Where?" I followed them into the area. We packed together like rats in a cage staring into one of the corner rooms. Everyone turned off their flashlight. Irregular breathing filled the stale air. I noticed a small African American boy looking very frightened. I smiled at him.

"It's okay," I whispered down to him. "I won't let anything happen to you."

"I saw it to," he told me with big eyes. "I really did."

A few minutes ticked by. But no ghost show. I had missed it. A few lingering people came down into the area, while a few headed to the exit. I went with them, seeing them off. The little boy came down the hallway and asked to stand with me.

"Of course," I said to him.

"I'm scared," he told me.

"When you're scared, just pray," I told him. "You'll feel better."

Then came footsteps, shrieks and horror filled cries. The group in the back came running out of the back room.

"Screw this," one man yelled.

"Good luck to you," another yelled to me.

About ten people rushed by me, trying to pack into the stairwell all at once. The stairs became alive with the pounding of their feet.

"What did you see?" I said as they flew by me. I had never seen people disappear so fast.

"It was a woman," someone answered. "Or half of one. We could see her shoulder, hand and arm."

"What was she wearing?"

"She was wearing white," came several rushed answers as the bodies disappeared down the staircase. "She looked like a nurse."

Within seconds, I was standing alone in the hallway. Me, the nurse and the little girl. I felt chilled, shaken. Two

CHAPTER 8

customers straggled into my hallway, walking into the back celled rooms where the nurse had just been seen. I didn't say anything, waiting to see if they would also come screaming out. But they didn't.

Lori came over to my side of the building. Mayflower was closing. Soon Sean joined us.

"I finally saw something," Sean said to me.

"What?"

"I went out on break and I was near one of the empty buildings," he said. "When I flashed my light across one of the buildings, there was a large, dark shadow inside."

"I believe it," I told him. I then told him what happened only minutes earlier.

"Oh, I heard about it," Sean said. "They were out front talking about it."

"Goodnight, Mayflower," I said to the dark hallway. "Don't anyone follow me home."

I trailed Sean down to the first floor and out the main doorway.

"So just how many ghosts live in the Mayflower," I asked the head security guard, an elderly gentleman who sported a no nonsense attitude.

"There are two confirmed ghosts," he replied. "A woman and a little girl."

"There is another," I told him. "It's a man and he stays in the common room."

But I had to wonder if there were a lot more. Perhaps they used the tunnels and just traveled around from building to building.

I wondered what Friday would hold and would I have the nerve to set foot back into the Mayflower building.

Friday, October 21, 2011

Friday night I had arrived at Pennhurst early. I spent some time walking around the walkway and looking at the other buildings. I wondered which of the buildings Sean had seen a shadow. Once again, the crowds started rolling in and the lines quickly filled. Ghouls and staff members of Pennhurst rushed around, getting into place and directing the crowds.

Before our building opened, Lori and I spent a few minutes talking in the larger hallway on the second floor of Mayflower. We were discussing the previous weekend and how we were going to deal with the crowds and issues we knew would arise.

We were standing next to the glassless window, deep in conversation, only about two feet apart. No one else was on the floor with us. In the middle of our words, a whistle blew softly between us. We both froze.

"Did you hear that?" I asked her, knowing she was hard of hearing.

"Yes," she replied, eyes wide.

"Looks like someone is listening in on us," I said, glancing around the area. But no one was there. The sound had been to close for comfort. In my mind, I imagined it to be shadow man from the common room. We were near his domain.

Someone yelled up the main staircase that customers were starting to enter the building. But the ghostly whistler remained in my thoughts.

Lori and I were now into a good routine on the second floor and we backed each other up. People came in larger groups and the Mayflower was filled with the sound of their excitement and screams.

CHAPTER 8

Chains were often broken as people would lean into them and innocently walk into the various cells. Lori and I spent a lot of time fixing the chains and chasing people out of the rooms.

Some people would sit in the common room on the old rubber chairs. I had to wonder if these folks could see the chairs in the daylight if they would still sit on them. The chairs were less than appealing. People were still capturing pictures of shadow man in the common room. In one particular picture, a group of people had been sitting around the table. In the background, the shadow of a man appeared to loom over the group. I had to wonder why shadow man preferred the common room. Did he ever leave it?

Once again, people made claims that they had seen the little girl. Over the past few weekends, she had been seen in just about every cell on the second floor. I had to wonder if she was walking by me in the hallway to get to the various rooms. But why hadn't I seen her? I had been in Mayflower for weeks.

Someone else reported a woman had hummed into his ear. The man was really spooked because no one had been around him.

"Sounds like the nurse was flirting with you," I said, smiling. "Lucky you."

More of my relatives arrived and explored Mayflower. My brother's girlfriend had gotten really sick to her stomach and ran out of Mayflower. When I looked out the windows, I was amazed by the size of the crowds. I barely talked to anyone, trying to keep the lines moving.

Clank. I heard the sound of a chain breaking in the common room. Once again, I left the larger hallway and went to see who was doing what.

A group of people were standing in the doorway of one of the common's room cells. They were just staring at a corner.

"Okay, who broke my chain?" I asked the group, making my way around them.

"Sorry," a dark hair girl said. "But there's something in there."

"I believe you," I told her. It was probably shadow man since we were in his realm.

"There is a quarter in the corner of the room," one man said. "It was spinning around by itself."

"Really," I said. I stood next to them, looking at the corner. I could make out the quarter, which was lying about a foot away from the corner wall. But it was flat, motionless.

The eager group was holding up the line as they waited anxiously for the quarter to do something, anything.

"Okay, folks," I said after a few moments. "I need to put the chain back up. Someone probably threw the quarter into the room. I can tell you that there wasn't a quarter in there earlier."

I went inside the room and looked at the quarter. It was new and shiny, hardly a ghostly apparition. Perhaps had the quarter been old, worn, I would have wondered. But I left the coin in the corner for shadow man to play with and chained the doorway, returning to my post.

Disappointed, the group moved along.

It was a great night for ghost hunting. A lot of people claimed it was their second trip to the Mayflower. Most had something happened to them weeks earlier and came back for another meeting with the dead. Some claimed Howie's plane had moved from its earlier spot. I wasn't sure, since I hadn't really taken notice.

The night deepened as the hours crept past midnight. But at least I had something to sit on. Earlier in the day, I bought

CHAPTER 8

myself a portable stool from Walmart and was glad for the decision to do so. It was great to get off my feet, if only for a few minutes. Normally, I liked being eye to eye with the people. But my feet hurt from standing long hours. Lori was having the same problem but started wearing special boots, which seemed to work for her. The stool was a blessing and worth the few bucks to buy it.

I was a bit disappointed in the amount of ghostly activity. For some reason I thought that the closer to Halloween we got, the more the paranormal activity would increase. I didn't realize that I had assumed this until later in the evening. So I stuck to my same stories, hoping to excite people and give them some kind of scare. But a lot of people were disappointed not to experience or see any ghosts.

It was as if all the spirits had taken a break for the evening. Perhaps they were sick of the crowds. Even shadow man seemed overly quiet.

But Saturday night the spirits came back and with a vengeance.

Saturday, October 22, 2011

Saturday evening had a strange feeling when I entered the Mayflower building. Something lingered in the atmosphere. It was heaviness. I could feel pressure around me. The front door orderlies, Mitch and his wife were huddled together, talking. Mitch handed me a flashlight to use. Mitch told me his wife was feeling sick. He wasn't sure how long she would last. He also told me he was also feeling ill. I gave Mitch an Advil for his headache. I went upstairs wondering if we were all getting sick from the damp, cold air. I felt a bit funny in my head as well. Not exactly sick, but a bit foggy brained. People started entering the building. But it wasn't long when Lori came over to me looking pale and miserable.

"I'm sick," she said. Misery hung in her eyes.

"What's the matter?"

"I don't know," Lori said. "I feel like I'm going to faint. I almost lost my balance and fell. I'm sorry, but I got to leave."

"I understand," I replied. Lori went into details how she suddenly felt faint. I could tell by her ashen complexion, she was a shaken by her symptoms. "Drive home carefully."

After Lori left, I was alone on the floor. Extra help was supposed to arrive on my floor. But no one came. I began watching the entire floor, constantly moving to check on all the three staircases. It was a difficult task and people took advantage, sneaking under the chains. The crowds increased in numbers but then came the smaller groups. A long pause would follow when I was alone on the floor. Something was watching me. It was unnerving, eerie - in some ways threatening.

A woman came into the larger hallway. She had something on her phone and was excitedly showing it around to the people in her group. I went over to see what all the excitement was about.

"I got a picture of a man," she said, quickly flashing a photo in front of me.

I gasped. It was a ghoulish image of a man, but his eyes were hollow, black. I had seen a lot of photos, but this one unnerved me. Fear lurked around my heart. I realized that the thing was on the same floor with me. "Where…where did you take it?"

"Right there," she said, pointing to the common room. "Near the bathroom."

I shouldn't have even asked. I knew where shadow man liked to hang out. He was always in or near the bathroom,

CHAPTER 8

sometimes near the closets. Of all the pictures I had seen of him, this one had to be the most sinister. The photo rippled through my thoughts, taunting me with whom and what shadow man could be. The photo bothered me.

After she left, I found myself alone. I sat on my stool, staring into the room housing Howie's plane. It felt like something was standing inside the doorway, watching me. I stared back, humming and faking a false bravo. I held my flashlight and from time to time turned it on, lighting the area where I thought something stood.

I started feeling funny. I grew light headed, felt strange. I wondered if I would faint. I had only fainted once in my life. Now the sensation alarmed me. I shook my head, trying to shake the weird sensation. Then I turned on my flashlight, aiming it into Howie's room. Nothing. Still. I felt incredibly ill. It hit me all at once. Now I knew what Lori was talking about. I felt like I was under some kind of attack. It was weird. I said a quick prayer for protection from evil. Whatever it was, it was dark and definitely screwing with me. I knew it was the man I seen in the photo. Shadow man's image was still in my mind, messing with me. Fear lurked in my soul as I shakily tried to gain control, put up mental blocks and ward him off.

Mitch came up from downstairs. I was really glad to see him. Normally, I never took a break unless absolutely necessary. But I needed some air. I asked him to watch my spot. I hurried outside into the cold night. People were waiting in lines, eager to see the attractions. I hurried along the catwalk, breathing in the gulps of icy air. The portable toilets had a long line. I stood behind several women, who when spying my outfit, knew I worked at Pennhurst. Eagerly they began questioning me about which was the better attraction to go into since they only had money to go into one more.

GHOSTS OF MAYFLOWER

"If you want a good scare, go into the tunnels," I said half-heartedly. Anxiously, I stared at the Mayflower second floor windows, wondering how Mitch was doing in my spot. Maybe I should have warned him about shadow man.

My feet dragged as I returned to the Mayflower and cautiously entered the foyer. I rolled my eyes upward, prayed for protection from evil and then climbed the staircase to relieve Mitch. I was determined not to be scared away.

I suddenly realized that I wasn't sick anymore. In fact, I was back to my normal self. I took a deep breath and got angry that I was almost chased away by shadow man. I pasted a smile on my lips and began greeting people.

I still worked the second floor alone. But I was glad that I won the battle within myself. I began walking the hallways and told arriving people about the horrible picture of the man I had seen. I had to wonder how shadow man enjoyed my ghastly descriptions of him. The customers loved hearing about him.

As the night closed down, I thought about what had happened to me. There had been so many people over the past weekend that had felt ill in the Mayflower. The illness would suddenly hit them and then they would hurry out. Their symptoms were nausea and headaches. I didn't dwell or try to reason it out much. I could only wonder what Sunday would bring. It was supposed to snow and Ghost Hunters was stationed on the property.

Sunday, October 23rd

To my surprise on Sunday night, Lori came back at work. As sick as the poor woman had seemed, I was sure she would have been a no show. But I was glad to see her. I really didn't

CHAPTER 8

want to work the second floor alone now that I had a good look at shadow man.

I started handing out Halloween candy to the children. With Halloween approaching, I wanted to give them a treat for having the nerve to come through Mayflower. I mostly gave out M & M's or lollipops. The kids liked getting the treats and even a few adults asked me for some.

Once again, Sunday night brought out the same kind of crowd – mostly families. Every time, I walked down the main hallway, I would think of shadow man and his creepy image. I often paced the floor in between the scattered groups to keep warm and also to keep my feet moving. I was walking towards the middle staircase when I tripped over somebody sitting on the floor. I felt the thud of their soft body as my foot connected into their form. Instinctively, I glanced down to see who I'd hurt, an apology ready on my lips.

But no one was there. I just shook my head, unnerved. Even kicking a ghost was disheartening. Due to overcrowding, the past residents of Pennhurst had often sat on the floor.

Had I kicked a lost soul still lingering in the hallway? Now I walked the hallway with a tentative step.

October 27th, Thursday

It was a rotten night, cold and rainy. The parking was terrible because of the mud and the large puddles. The other problem was that the show *Ghost Hunters* was now on the property. They were getting ready for their Halloween live show. They had taken over one of our parking areas so we had to park in a different location. Normally, I wouldn't have cared, but the place was a muddy mess and

GHOSTS OF MAYFLOWER

it was a miserable walking to the Mayflower building. We all wondered if we would even get any customers. At first, there wasn't anyone in the lines outside. We orderlies stood just inside the foyer of the Mayflower building, talking and joking around. We told ghost stories and heard new ones. But then the customers came. Slowly at first, but still people trickled onto the walkways, entering the various attractions.

The Administration building got the first customers. Mayflower usually came afterwards. While we were watched and waited from our vantage point for the loyal patrons, our head security guard decided to tell us some really corny jokes. He was really into one when he yelled.

"Hey, something just walked across the hallway."

We all turned around, staring down the first floor hallway. No one was in the building but our small group and we were all accounted for. The elderly guard ran into the hallway, jerking on his flashlight. He quickly raced into several rooms, searching around. Slowly, we all followed. The guard came out, looking perplexed.

"I know what I say. It was a large dark shadow of a man walking across and into one of the rooms."

We all just looked at him. None of us were shocked. I think I can say that all of us orderlies had seen the shadows, pictures and heard the sounds of the Mayflower's dead. We were the last and remaining few that now worked in the building. Others had quit or were fired. This security guard was usually outside, lingering around the Administration building. He looked as shocked as I was the first time I experienced the paranormal in Mayflower.

People began coming into our building. I went upstairs with Lori and sat down my bag. It was damp and cold upstairs.

CHAPTER 8

The floors were wet in some areas. I had so many clothes on, I looked like a snowman in my white outfit. Both me and Lori had to wear gloves. Since it was Halloween weekend, I had bought more candy at the store to hand out to kids. The candy was stored in a black Halloween bag with a large orange pumpkin on the front of it. Inside, I had more bags of M&M's and another bag of lollipops. I felt bad for a lot of the kids that came through Mayflower. Some of them were terrified. They looked like they wanted to be anywhere else but in the building. Some of the kids were really young. But I usually got a large smile when I handed out the candy. More adults asked me for some. I would just laugh at them.

"Sorry, just for the kids," I said.

To my surprise, we had gotten really busy with groups. The floors became filthy from the muddy shoes. But people didn't care. They were having fun. So was I. A Chinese woman was really into taking photos on her phone. But then she got really excited. She was standing in line, staring at her phone. A small group huddled around her. Of course, I had to see as well.

"Can I see?" I asked, approaching her. With worried, eyes, she quickly held it in front of me. Of all the pictures, I had seen. This one was one of the strangest. There was a large, misty body sticking out of the wall in the main hallway. Arms, head, shoulders were all clearly visible. The other half of the body seemed to be stuck in the wall. I looked up at the spot on the wall where she gotten the shot. It had to be a good seven feet up from the ground. I was creeping out. This ghost had been hanging just above my head. It was a surreal moment. I spent the remainder of the evening, avoiding walking near that particular wall.

Halloween Weekend – Friday Night: October 28th, 2011

Excitement lingered in the air as I arrived at Pennhurst extra early. Halloween was on everyone's minds, due to arrive on Monday. Ghost Hunters was going to be filming live their Halloween special and everyone was aware of their presence on the property. I was hoping to catch a glimpse of them but had figured they were staying away because of the crowds. Sean wasn't working that night, so we had to improvise and rework the flashlight situation. I was now gathering the flashlights from the customers, placing them into a Halloween bucket that I had brought from home and then took turns with Mitch running them down to the first floor so he would have an ample supply for the arriving customers.

I had gotten the flashlights for a while, which could be a difficult ordeal because a lot of people would get attached to their flashlight and it would disappear into someone's coat pocket. I assumed people wanted a memento of being at the haunt and this was their way of obtaining something. So I tried to keep an eye on approaching patrons when they came into the large hallway and who had one of our flashlights. For the most part, people had been honest and handed the flashlight over to me.

For the first half of the night, we exited people down the main staircase and out the front door, but this could cause a jam up with arriving customers. But then we got some extra help and opened the middle staircase to exit the people.

I no longer had to get the flashlights. A security guard now stood at the bottom of the staircase and was gathering them. After a while, he called up to me that he needed a break and would I take his spot.

CHAPTER 8

Lori moved into my position and I moved to the bottom of the staircase to collect flashlights. I stood just outside the back doorway. It was cold standing in that spot. Across from me was the Quaker building. People would stop and stare at the building, often questioning me about it. Some claimed they were seeing strange lights in the windows.

I enjoyed the fresh air but the cold air prompting me inside the stairwell. I started collecting the flashlights in the small landing of the first floor. This had a closed doorway with a windowless window. I had a bird's eye view of the people on the first floor as they began their tour of Mayflower. I would look out the window as they passed. It wasn't long, before people would scream upon seeing me.

Usually a group would pass the door. But there was always that one special person who would walk to the door and look into the window. I would just stare at them. I always got a jump or scream. This was a lot of fun. I felt like a kid again. Pennhurst seemed to bring out my inner child. The wayward security guard arrived and I went back upstairs to the second floor and resumed my position in the large hallway.

People wanted to talk about ghosts.. I heard many tales of haunted houses. It seemed a lot of people had ghost troubles at home. I heard some really creepy stories about playful ghosts, some violent. I saw more photos of orbs, shadows and images taken in Mayflower. People wanted to know if I was working on Halloween? They wanted to know about Ghost Hunters and the up and coming show.

Saturday, October 29, 2011

Saturday night Mother Nature decided to pull her own trick of the season. Spring City and the surrounding areas had been affected by a freak snow storm. Due to the bad weather, Pennhurst had to be closed for the night. I was disappointed not to work but enjoyed spending the extra time with my kids. Since it was Halloween weekend, we watched Halloween specials on television and enjoyed playing out in the snow.

Sunday Night: Mischief Night

Mischief night was cold. A lot of the snow had melted off. But Pennhurst was open. Once again, I loaded up my candy bag to hand out treats to kids in the Mayflower. I had to dress in a lot of layers to stay warm, including wearing gloves.

Ghost Hunter's equipment was in place for their Halloween special. This equipment was foreign to me. People would ask me about it, but I have to say I was at loss of how it worked or even what it was. But I did notice that it was set up in the common room, near the rollaway closets and also in the back celled rooms, where the nurse and little girl hung out. I was curious about how ghost hunters knew which rooms to place the equipment. A security guard was placed in the common room to guard the equipment, since people were free to roam in the room. The other equipment was protected by a chain across the doorway and of course, me.

Mayflower felt really creepy. The coldness crept along my spine, chilling me. The cold of the concrete floor penetrated right through my double layered socks. Fogged breath filled the air. I chewed my gum and would shuffle around to stay warm.

After a time, a heavy set man stood next to me. His wife was looking over her shoulder towards the common room. Excitement filled her features as she turned towards me.

"There's a psychic boy talking to a ghost in the other room," she said.

CHAPTER 8

"What?" I immediately looked towards the common room. Slowly, I walked down the hallway, staring in through the windowless window. Sure enough, a young boy and his mother and father were standing near the bathroom. The mother and father were both leaning down as if listening to the boy speak. A small crowd had gathered around them, listening to what the boy was saying.

Shadow man. I was freaked out that this boy might be talking to him. The parents had no idea what he looked like. But I had a pretty good idea. I wanted to go into the common room and protect the child. I had no doubt that shadow man wasn't a good entity. But he stayed away from me and I him.

But I had to keep an eye on my hallway, the staircases and Ghost Hunter's equipment. I had no choice but to stay in my area. For if I didn't, people would take advantage and start wandering around or snapping chains.

As I was standing near the staircase, a large man approached me. He had ghost recording equipment in his hands. These items, I had seen over the past few weeks but his looked exsepensive and he was busy reading its screen. He stopped to speak to me, mentioning the child in the other room talking to children's spirits.

"How do you know it's a child?" I asked him.

"Well wasn't that who lived in here?" he asked me. He sized me up as only a ghost expert would do.

"It was a men's ward," I said.

"That so," he said. "Well I am a ghost hunter. You might have heard of me." He rattled off his name and his expertise.

No, I hadn't heard of him. And for the life of me, I can't even remember where he had said he was from or the name of his business. But he claimed to be a paranormal expert. He seemed very pleased by the psychic boy's ability. But you

GHOSTS OF MAYFLOWER

didn't have to be psychic to have the ghosts of Mayflower messing with you.

"Not all of the ghosts in this building are good," I told him. "In fact, some are really bad."

He didn't like my statement, once again, giving me a once over as if I was a fool. Perhaps I was. I usually kept my opinions to myself, but this guy was a bit much. Then he demanded to know my name. So I told him and he nodded and walked down the staircase.

As I turned around, a little boy was approaching me. He was really cute and looked really young - the psychic boy.

His mother prodded him along until the boy stood by me. His father hung behind them and then entered the stairwell. He went down to the first landing and leaned against the wall, staring up at his wife, me and his son.

"My son's psychic," the woman said to me. A huge smile filled her face. She was obviously very proud of the fact.

I looked down at the boy, who stared up at me with sad eyes.

"Would you like some M'M's?" I asked him, hoping to bring a smile to his face.

He shook his head no.

The boy's mother began rattling off a list of things the boy could do. He could speak to spirits. She just knew he was psychic.

"He was speaking to a child in the other room," the mother said. "Weren't you?"

The boy looked at her, then at me. He touched his cheek. "Something kissed me on my cheek."

"The spirits fight over my son," the woman gushed. "At night when he's sleeping, they grab his arms and play tug of war with his body. He gets yanked all over the bed."

CHAPTER 8

"Well that's not a good thing," I replied, horrified. "It sounds like you need divine intervention."

"Perhaps," she said. But her smiling face revealed a different scenario. She liked her boy being special.

The little boy looked up at me with large eyes.

"How old are you?" I asked him.

"Four," he replied. Then he looked around as if suddenly aware of where he was. "Is this place really haunted? Are there ghosts in here?"

I patted him on the head. "Honey, you are safe in here. Nothing will harm you."

But as I was saying this, his mother quickly leaned down to him. "Yes. Yes, there are ghosts in here."

The boy's eyes filled with tears. "I want my daddy." He quickly ran down the staircase to his father, who looked about ready to blow up.

"I would take your son to Sunday school," I told the father, who shrugged and took his son down the remaining staircase.

"Well, maybe we should," his mother finally said. "I thought about it."

"It's the only way to get rid of evil," I told her. "I know what I am talking about."

"It was nice talking with you," she said, smiling.

After she left, I thought about the boy. How could the poor little thing sleep at night? I felt pity for him and prayed for him. I'm wasn't trying to push my Christian beliefs on anyone, but they are part of who I am.

My thoughts turned to my own childhood. When I was four, my parents moved into a new house. I was given a bedroom of my own. Or so I had thought. For a time, I shared it with the ghost of a man. I saw him twice and would often hear his footsteps as he walked around at night. No one else

GHOSTS OF MAYFLOWER

in my house seemed to be affected by him. I often saw shadows, faces. I had invisible friends. I dreamed events before they happened and would just know things about people.

The last time I saw the ghost from my childhood, I was sixteen. I saw him walk into my parents' garage and disappear. I was older. Braver. He didn't scare me as he once had. These things that have happened to me, I don't usually talk about. People look at you strange and I prefer the living.

I have learned to put up block walls.

As the evening wore down, Lori came over to my side of the building. There were just a few lingering customers. A group of people came up the staircase. A dark haired woman walked past me, into the large hallway.

She stared around at the ceiling and said, "hello" to me.

"They like singing," she said looking at me.

I realized she was a psychic, doing a reading. At first, I didn't recognize the other people, who had clipboards in their hands and seemed to be studying the floor.

The psychic rattled off a song she said they liked hearing the most.

I had to smile. I was always singing in Mayflower – mostly when I was alone. "I don't know that song," I replied, hoping some entity wasn't given me a song request.

Then a tall lanky man entered the hallway. I immediately recognized him as Ben Hanson, from Fact or Fiction. Apparently, they were also part of the ghost hunter's special.

Ben introduced himself to me and then the others. He asked me what I had seen in Mayflower. I told him.

"Good," Ben said. "We got the cameras in the right place."

I was then shown a photo from a laptop.

"Is this who you have seen in the common room?" Ben asked.

CHAPTER 8

"That's him" I replied, staring at the ghoulish image of shadow man. "I've seen a lot of pictures of him – mostly shadows."

I asked for a photo and Ben complied. I told him, I enjoyed watching his show. After a few minutes of talking with him, Lori and I were released for the night. We weren't working on Halloween, but I was really curious as to what Ghost Hunter's would find at Pennhurst and couldn't wait to see the show.

Figure 5. Ben Hanson, Fact or Fiction 2011

◄ GHOSTS OF MAYFLOWER

Friday after Halloween. November 4th, 2011

On Friday evening, I wondered if Pennhurst would draw an after Halloween crowd. I shouldn't have worried. There was plenty of thrill seekers. The ghost tour of the Mayflower building was busy. I worked the larger of the hallways, exiting the people down the middle stairwell. The building was cold. I had dressed in several layers of clothing. I think if I would have added one more layer, I would have resembled a snowman.

Lori worked the floor with me. She stayed in the back area off my hallway. I was impressed by her nerve. Out of all the places on our floor, this area seemed to be the most paranormal. I often told people that the nurse and the little girl hung back there. People got touched, tickled or heard noises in the area. And it was the place a group of people had come face to face with the nurse, screaming in terror as they ran past me and down into the stairwell.

As I was standing in the hallway, something black swooped down in front of me. I screamed, drawing stares from the people in line. They all looked up. Then it happened again. A bat. A big bat with wide wings. When he made a showing, he was quick about it, disappearing as if into thin air. Three times he startled me. Three times I yelled. Lori laughed at me. After doing some investigating, Lori discovered the bat was hiding out in the bathroom off the common room.

A lot of people that came into the Mayflower wanted to know exactly where the Ghost Hunter's had filmed. I pointed them out the common room filing cabinet area. Eagerly, they explored the area, taking pictures with their cell phones.

As the evening progressed, I saw little in the way of paranormal activity. Perhaps the ghosts were as cold as I. But then

CHAPTER 8

a group of people came through. They eagerly showed me a photo they took in the common room. Several people were in the photo, standing around a table. But over the shoulder of one woman, a black silhouette of a head was clearly visible. I recognized him as the shadow man. I had seen him a lot in the common room, either with my own eyes, others accounts or in many of the photographs.

I handed out bags of M & M's to the kids that came through. I thought about how the Ghost's Hunters had used candy to try and lure out any ghostly kids seeking a treat. Several teens came through. One with a stunning Mohawk of sorts.

One African American woman walked passed me in the opposite line. She leaned close to me. "Has anyone been holding or touching your hand tonight?"

"Not lately," I replied, smiling.

"Something keeps holding mine," she said. She wore a faint worried grin. Her friends obviously didn't believe her, making fun of her claims.

I watched the group walk into Lori's area. I had found in working that spot, that most people who are being touched have had the experience in that location. I was right. The women came towards the exit.

"Something is following me," the young woman said. This time she looked worried. "I think something whispered something to me."

"Well it better not follow you home," one of the other women piped up. She was clearly distressed over the idea.

"Just tell it to stay here," I say. "That it's not allowed to come home with you."

This works for the women, who clearly yelled out, "Don't come home with us." They hurried down the staircase, and I wondered how they'd fair in the tunnels.

Other people captured orbs in their photos. One man has an impressive image of a large line, looking like a shooting star. I urged them to share any photos on the Pennhurst face book page.

Another group of young men came in. They entered into Lori's area and hung out for a few minutes. Then one screamed and then all came running out towards me.

"I'm getting out of here," one man cried, rushing into the stairwell.

"What happened, "I asked.

"Something was whispering to us," the group replied.

"Well what did it say?"

"We couldn't make it out," came the reply. "It was garbled." The group hurried out.

Others hearing the tale, eagerly went into the same area, trying to listen to the voice. A short time later, several emerged disappointed not to have heard anything.

As the night winded down, Lori left her area to get ready to leave. I told Sean about the whispering.

"Let's check it out," he said.

Feeling courageous, I followed him into the darkness. Over the past few weekends, I had felt accepted in the building. We walked back into the area, sat on the desk and turned off our flashlights. Several minutes passed. Nothing.

"Just as I thought," Sean said.

I just shrugged and followed him out.

November 5 2011, Saturday

The cold was really getting to me. I could feel the damp, icy chill seeping up from the floors of the Mayflower building. It lingered in my knee, crept up my leg and gave my right

CHAPTER 8

knee a jab, then the throbbing began. A few years ago, I had fallen on some ice and pulled a ligament in my knee. After an operation, the knee had almost returned to normal, but arthritis was almost a given. The doctor warned me of it. I had hoped I still had more time for the inevitable. Not so.

Earlier in the night, Sean and I had a disagreement. After he left the area, I felt angry energy surrounding me. The sensation was odd. It was like something was mad we'd argued. The feeling was strong, overbearing. I thought that I was imagining it, until the first customers arrived. In the very first group, a young man told me something shoved him hard in the common room. This guy seemed very happy by this. The woman next to him smiled and said, "Something in here is really angry."

I strived to put my argument with Sean to rest, put on a false smile. It takes a little time, but I loosened up. Lori decided to stay in the back rooms off my hallway. From time to time, she left her area to check on chains and any mischief brewing. I did the same when I got breaks in the lines.

People arrived in droves. They know it's the last Saturday of the Pennhurst Haunt until next year. After tonight, we will only be open for two more nights. I began to notice their hats. Because of the cold, everyone was bundled more for sleighing then ghost hunting. All sorts of hats appeared. There was the usual baseball cap. But then there are knit or wooly hats. Some resemble Eskimos with their thick fur linings and long draw strings. These are usually gray or brown. But it's the animal ones that stood out. People of all ages sport the hats. Some have bears, raccoons or animals of unknown origin. One tall gentleman had a bear of the top of his head. When he exited into the staircase, a white polar bear with beady eyes stared back at me. Two long paws hung down his back as if giving him a warm hug.

GHOSTS OF MAYFLOWER

A small woman appeared, approaching out of the dark like a freaky spectacle. On her head, she wore what looked like glowing tentacles. They stick out in every direction. She was an elderly woman, who was really enjoying herself. I looked at her and smiled.

"That's the craziest thing I've seen all night," I told her.

"Thanks," she replied, pleased by my comment.

The line came in long segments, followed by a few paused minutes. During this time, a few stragglers had the opportunity to explore in the quieter atmosphere. These are the people, I closely watched. It's the smaller groups that have interaction with the ghosts.

A man came rushing out of the back area with his girlfriend following. Lori had just left the area, checking out the floor.

"A woman just moaned," the man told me. Alarm was in his eyes.

"Did you hear it?" I asked his companion.

"I heard something, but wasn't sure what it was."

I told them about the nurse that liked to be in the back rooms. This alarmed the man, but excited the woman. She wanted to hang out longer, but he prevailed and they left.

Another woman in line told me she had seen the little girl in the front rooms. She claims she was psychic and she has the gift of sight.

Talk still lingered amongst the crowd about the Ghost Hunters and the Ghost Hunter television special. They eagerly tried to guess what areas were most explored. From time to time, I helped people out and pointed to the areas of interest.

People get rowdier over a period of time. Alcohol usually lingered around the boisterous groups. I had to chase several people out of the common room. One man was hiding

CHAPTER 8

beneath a desk, making horrible banging noises. Four times I had to fix the same broken chain, chasing people out the same area. Some people slammed the filing cabinets doors, shoved tables and pushed furniture around. I managed to patrol the area and yet still watched the doorways. When the crowed line broke the hallway chain, they flowed out into the area, suddenly free. I herded them back into place.

For the most part, I really enjoyed watching people. I liked watching their reactions, seeing their faces. Talking with them when I could. I got a lot of questions, ones that are all too familiar to me. "Why can't they go to the third floor? Where are the ghosts? Did anything ever happen to me?"

I kept my answers simple. When the lines are thick, I needed to do this or the line will stall by a particular room. But when there are just a few people in line, I told them what they wanted to know, pointing out areas of activity.

A young couple hung around my hallway, stalling at every room. The woman was short with eyebrow piercings. She wore her hair tied back into a bun. The man stared longingly at Howie's airplane before they disappeared into the back rooms.

The lines started to drop in numbers. People were more scattered. There were times I was alone while Lori walked the floors. From time to time, she exited our floor and went to the first, took a walk through and came up the back staircase.

Another couple came through. They looked closer to my age. The lady had a long pony tail tied up in a clip. When they came out of the back rooms, her pony tail was hanging along her shoulder. She fingered it, uncertainty on her features. I know what she's going to say, but still I asked.

"Is everything alright?"

"Something just yanked on my hair," she replied. "Hard. My clip went flying off."

"I believe you," I replied. How could I not when so many people have made the same claim. All in the same area.

The woman and husband then told me how their house was haunted by a little girl. They said how mean she was and how she didn't like the husband. The little girl liked to throw things around, mostly items in the cupboards.

"She isn't very nice," the woman says.

"Sounds like it," I replied. "Are you sure it's a little girl?"

"I saw her. It's a little girl. We live in an old farmhouse but can't find any records of any children dying in the house. There is also a teenager that comes through. He was killed in the neighbor's front yard. He doesn't do much. But we saw his shadow."

They were so sincere it would be hard not to believe them. After they left, the woman with the brow piercing emerged from the back.

"Something grabbed my bun," she said, touching the short springy hair.

"I believe it," I said. "There was another woman who just left. She said her hair had been pulled."

The couple stood beside me. They loved being in the Mayflower, evident by their happy faces. They told me that they have come all the way from Virginia just to see the place. It took them six hours one way and they were returning home that same night.

"Well thank you for visiting us," I replied, impressed. The furthest I had ever traveled for a Halloween fright was within an hour's ride.

"You're welcome," the woman replied. "We're going to make it an annual event."

They hung around, talking to me about the history of the Mayflower. Since I was writing about working at Pennhurst, I

CHAPTER 8

had a few facts that I shared. It's the part I liked most about the job, hearing other people's thoughts while trying to maintain an unbiased opinion.

Another woman approached from the back area. Once again, she had a ponytail. The look on her face told a familiar tale.

"Something pulled my hair," the woman said.

"Something pulled mine," the brow pierced woman added.

"You're the third one in a row," I said, smiling as if congratulating her on some kind of achievement.

The last group came through, all of it men. One of them had a short pony tail. I watched them enter the back area, wondering if the man would get his hair yanked. But it was not to be. They emerged unscathed. It seemed that mostly women were touched, making me wonder who was doing the hair pulling. Could it be a man instead of the nurse?

The night closed down without further incident. My feet were so cold, my toes were numb. Stiffly, I followed Lori down the main staircase, clocked out and was thankful for the heat in my car. When I got home, I was told that a man's shadow had been seen at my house at least three times during the evening. Twice by my son's girlfriend. The other by my daughter.

I worried what I might have brought home with me from the Mayflower and take my fears to prayer. If something had followed me home, it had to go back. It was not allowed to stay.

Sunday, November 6, 2011

Arriving at Pennhurst, all employees were ordered to meet in front of the Administration building at six o'clock for a meeting. We looked like a strange bunch of people standing there. Some were in costume, some half-dressed. Cigarette smoke billowed through the crowd of over 80 people. The meeting was brief, relaying how important the coming Friday night was to Pennhurst. We were going to have a lot of VIP's and we needed to give a good performance. Everyone was in good form and cheered at the praise we received. But I think a few were a bit saddened that the season was coming to a close. When we were dismissed, I returned with Lori to take our spots on the second floor of the Mayflower.

The cold air did nothing to stop customers from arriving promptly at six thirty. I took a few minutes during their arrival and took a few pictures of some of the rooms in the Mayflower. Most of the night, I worked the second floor with Lori, only leaving it once to take an employee's spot below, who needed a trip to the bathroom.

The spot I filled was the first floor exit. There I collected flashlights, bid people goodnight and stared across at the Quaker building. An eerie glow emanated from one of the second floor windows. The beacon light flashed across the brick surface, but I couldn't figure out where the light could enter the domain. The Quaker building was supposedly one of the most active of all the buildings at Pennhurst. It had once housed some of the most violent of patients. I had watched old news footage from the 1960's. A young boy had been punished and had to spend time in the Quaker building to degrade him. It was said that patients that could speak would stop talking when staying in the building.

The stars overhead lit the sky in a cheery display amongst the gloomy feel of Pennhurst. As I stared a shooting star shot across the back of the Quaker building. The trees stirred in the cold breeze as leaves scattered across the parking lot. Finally the attendant returned and I was glad to get out of the wind.

CHAPTER 8

Sunday night was mostly quiet. Perhaps the ghosts were as cold as I. People would complain by the door that they didn't see anything. I assured them that the place was really haunted, but I had no control over the ghosts or activity. Several looked up claiming that if they could only get to the third floor, they would find some ghosts. Perhaps they were right.

A few customers had hair pulled or a coat tugged. But mostly pictures were empty of orbs. If I didn't know better, I'd wonder if the place was really haunted. That all changed when I got my pictures back the next day. I had taken a picture of the mirror in the second floor bathroom. I had seen a picture on the Pennhurst face book page of the same mirror with a woman standing in it. So I took one myself. But the image I got was not that of a woman, but of a strange looking monster like thing. It was really strange and I decided not to share it with my kids. They were already spooked over the picture I had taken on my front yard so I didn't want to push it.

I have decided to take a few more photos on Friday night to compare with my mirror ghoul. But no matter what, it was one of the creepiest pictures I had taken so far.

CHAPTER 9

Friday, November 11, 2011

FRIDAY EVENING WAS the final night at the Pennhurst Haunt 2011 season. It was a VIP night with a lot of specially invited guests. These groups were media related and some were from other haunts. But the groups coming up to the 2nd floor of the Mayflower were in indiscernible for the most part. Some individuals wore coats or jackets with their telltale markings. I recognized a few of the names, but others were foreign to me. Other haunts logos were quite interesting to see. There were also a lot of people wearing the Pennhurst shirts or jackets with the Pennhurst logo.

I decided to have fun with the crowds walking through and made sure I warned them to watch out for the nurse who gave shots.

It wasn't long into the evening before the first woman got her needle jab along with her daughter. They were standing off the main hallway, near the back cells. They came up to me, stunned with disbelief. I told them about the angry nurse. The younger girl was rubbing her neck. "Ow. That hurt. I hate needles."

"You'll be fine," I told her.

CHAPTER 9

"Maybe the nurse thought you needed your flu shot," the mother replied.

These women weren't scared, just stunned something had happened to them. Unlike other people, tonight's crowd wanted more action and hung in the back areas trying to interact more with the ghosts.

Things began to happen to a lot of various individuals. One man had his hair fingered. Another had a tug on his jeans. One guy had a voice recording of a something garbled from the first floors.

Two well-dressed ladies quickly shared a photo from the first floor with me. One woman had taken a picture of the other in front of one of the cells. In the background, the windows stood out in the gloomy atmosphere. On the floor was a picture of two spirits seemingly sitting on the floor, leaning against the wall. Their faces were vague, but I could clearly see their legs and forms.

Another photo I saw was that of a ghostly leg and foot, also taken on the first floor. A photographer from the Pennhurst Crew came in. I recognized the two girls from earlier times. They stopped to chat with me.

"Take a picture of the bathroom mirror," I told the girl holding the large camera. "See what you get."

She did and was stunned by the ghoulish face she got. She took a few more. All had weird images.

"Is there something in the mirror making it do that?" she asked me.

"Not that I can see," I told her. I had taken a closer look at the mirror earlier in the evening. The mirror was old and a bit distorted. But I hadn't seen any images or markings that would create such a ghoulish face. The young woman got very excited with her find and couldn't wait to show it to the owner

GHOSTS OF MAYFLOWER

of Pennhurst. She then went through her photos and showed me an eerie image of a tree stump or weed that looked like a freakish ghoul. It was located in the employee parking lot.

After the women left, the night was just beginning to stir with activity. A heavy woman got jabbed in her leg. I told her she got the dreaded shot. The man with her took a picture of the back of her leg, which bore a faint scratch. Over the course of the night, two more people received the needle in their shoulders. When I had a lull in people, I took a few pictures of the bathroom mirror to see what I'd find. I used a disposable camera. But later when I got the film developed, my film was ruined. My pictures were nothing but blurs – typical for most folks.

I would miss my job working in the Mayflower. I really liked talking to people and seeing their reactions to the happenings around them. I felt bad for the groups that had nothing happen to them and were bitterly disappointed. I would assure them that there were plenty of ghosts outside, especially in the tunnels. This usually perked them up as they eagerly went in search of their next thrill.

I saw a few familiar faces. People were returning to the Mayflower, having visited on other nights. These individuals would recognize me and quickly informed me they returned. Usually these customers had something happen to them on an earlier visit and they wanted more of the same.

A few children came through my floor. Most didn't seem too happy to be there, clinging to their parents. One fearless boy stomped his foot by every door. I often asked the kids if they saw any ghosts. Most of them said, "No." I would smile, pat them on their head and say, "That's probably a good thing since your parents would probably like to get some sleep tonight."

CHAPTER 9

The groups became sparse. I followed a few of them into the back area, watching them talk and look into the cells. One man came through with a voice recorder. He and his female companion read the names down the side wall of the first cell on the left. When they came to a certain name, a voice responded on the machine. I was fascinated. They quickly told me they figured out a man named Fisher was haunting the floors. Perhaps that was shadow man's real name.

I moved around the hallway, talking to different guest. All of a sudden, the man and woman with the voice recorder began screaming, rushing out of the back area towards me.

"We saw him. We saw him," they exclaimed.

"Who?"

"Fisher," the man said. "The voice recording said *manifestation* and then he appeared, standing along the wall."

"What did he look like," I asked, following them towards the cell. I peeked in, flashing my light on the area.

"He was wearing a dark suit," the woman said. "We could see his white cuffs."

Overhearing the news about Fisher, more people came around us, trying to peer into the cell to see Fisher. But nothing appeared.

Fisher was elusive. But then shadow man was good at his hiding games. I finally returned back into the larger hallway. Another group came through and entered the back hallway where Fisher had been spotted. They all came screaming out into the hallway, saying they saw a man in one of the rooms.

Once again, I went to see for myself. This time the man was seen in the opposite cell from the earlier sighting. I waited with the group. We all turned off our flashlights. Except for the sound of excited breathing, the group was hushed, eyes straining. We all stared into the cell. I couldn't see very well over some of their heads. Now and then someone would cry out. "Look. There he is. He's moving from side to side."

Several people jumped behind me. Others got too scared and left. Finally, I was with just a few brave souls, staring into the dark room. Nothing.

"Where did he go?" one woman asked. "He was just here."

I had a sneaking suspicion shadow man was hiding from me Perhaps he knew I was writing about him and didn't want to scare me off. Or perhaps my prayers were working only too well. At least that was my theory.

"He doesn't like me to see him," I said, putting my theory to the test. "I'll walk away and see if he comes back."

Slowly, I walked away towards the middle exit. Behind me the groups began to exclaim, "There he is. He's back."

Unsure of my strange reasoning, I returned to hanging out with the final groups. Mitch came up from the first floor and got into the action of trying to find the elusive shadow man. After a time, the groups finally dispersed and were replaced with new ones.

Another group cried out that they saw the little girl. One woman was pointing inside one of the cells. "There she is. See her."

I went to look. Nothing.

"I don't understand," the woman said looking at me. "She was just there and now she's not. Something scared her off."

I sighed and walked out. I worked eight weekends and I have never seen the little girl. Not that I wanted to. I had seen her in pictures. She was really tiny. Just about three foot high, dressed in wispy white.

The night began winding down. I took the time to study things on the 2nd floor so I could remember it. I took a long

CHAPTER 9

look at Howie's plane. It was a sad little plane, old and neglected. I wondered who had last played with it?

As we exited the building, I was filled with regret that I hadn't explored the building more. But I just didn't have the time. I would have liked to spend some time alone in the Mayflower. It was amazing that I could even want to because earlier in the season the building terrified me. I would never have wandered around alone. But somewhere along the line, my fears had disappeared. If there were truly lost souls inside the rooms, I felt compassion and sadness for their endless plight of cold darkness. But eternity is not mine to judge. I have no control of where people end up. It's just not my call.

I walked through the administration building, staring at the tall ceilings and ornate woodwork. It must have been something when it was first new, polished and freshly painted. But it was hard to envision.

Since Sean wasn't working the final night, I climbed into my cold car alone. I stared across the parking lot at the Quaker building. Weeds and overgrowth reflected in the bright moonlight. I pulled away into the night.

"No one is allowed to come home with me," I said over my shoulder, staring at my back seat. I smiled and shook my head.

CHAPTER 10

Party

THE FOLLOWING SATURDAY, Pennhurst held an employee party at Pennhurst. I took my daughter along with me since my husband was working. It was cold and sunny when we first arrived at Pennhurst. We parked behind the Mayflower building and I got a good look at the Quaker building in the daylight. It looked gloomy and overgrown, desolate. The walkway behind Quaker was laden with weeds and vines. It was hauntingly beautiful in its own way. I resisted the urge to follow the walkway to see where it led.

A huge bonfire was being prepared in the pavilion area. Families sat at the tables, while other conversed around the fire pit. I spent time talking to Lori and her husband, then to Mitch and his wife. I took my daughter into the Pennhurst store and bought several sweatshirts with the *Fear Is Real* logo.

James came out of the crowd and hugged me.

"I really missed you," I told him. "Where have you been working?"

"I was the bee keeper in the tunnels," he told me, smiling.

"Was it scary down there?"

"Yes," he said. "But I got through it."

CHAPTER 10

"Think you'll work here next year?" I asked him.

"Definitely," he replied.

I talked to James for a bit, and then went with my daughter to explore the Mayflower and take a few photos. I had been disappointed with my last photographs. I had been determined to catch a ghost on film. This was my last chance.

My daughter seemed a bit worried about the idea of taking pictures. She didn't want to go into the Mayflower building. We walked the walkway towards the Mayflower building and exited down into the parking lot by my car. I took a few photos of the front of the Quaker building and then the rear of Mayflower.

Shadows deepened as night was descending. I hurried to take a last peek at Mayflower before it got too dark to see inside the building.

My daughter and I entered the Mayflower foyer. Another employee with his kids came by us. They eagerly went upstairs to explore. Soon they came down and left the building. We were alone.

My daughter refused to go any farther than the foyer. I walked around the first floor, trying to keep a mental image of what I was seeing. I wasn't that familiar with the first floor, since I mainly worked the second. There were similarities, but then some differences. Unlike the second floor, real metal beds were in the cells, not just mattresses on the floors. There was also more furniture. I snapped a few pictures.

My daughter called for me to come back. I returned to her and tried to get her to go upstairs with me.

"No," she said. "I don't like it in here."

"I'll keep you safe," I told her. "You got nothing to worry about."

A familiar face appeared in the front door. It was

GHOSTS OF MAYFLOWER

Martha, the former resident that I had driven home weeks ago in the Pennhurst car. When she spied us, she begged us to go up to the second floor with her so she could get a picture.

Reluctantly, my daughter accompanied us. Martha snapped several photos and then we all returned downstairs.

"Are you trying to get a picture of a ghost?" I asked her.

"Oh no, honey," Martha said. "There aren't any ghosts in here. That's just a bunch of hype."

Just as Martha was saying this, my daughter snapped a picture with her cell phone. She had taken a picture of the top of the staircase leading down into the tunnel. We talked to Martha for a little longer and followed her out onto the walkway to see her off.

After Martha left us, my daughter stared down at the photo on her phone. I looked at it too.

"It looks like something is in your picture," I said, puzzled. "Can you enlarge it?"

My daughter enlarged the image. We both stared and stared. Moments ticked away as I waited to see what my daughter would say.

"There's a boy in my photo," my daughter said. She looked at me with large, scared eyes. "I can see him."

"I see him," I told her. I was as stunned as she.

An image of a half a boy's body was clearly visible in the lower right hand corner of the photograph. I thought he looked like he was twelve, thirteen. You could see his face and shoulders. He was wearing a dark suit and a whilte collared shirt. Next to him, I could see the wispy image of the little girl. I grew excited, my daughter alarmed.

"Now my phone is haunted," she said. "I want to erase it and get him off of it."

CHAPTER 10

"E-mail it to me," I told her. She did so, but the image wasn't as clear as on her phone. Still, it was spooky and unexplainable. Finally, I had an image of a ghost, not just orbs.

We decided to call the boy Thomas. The name popped in my head, so I stuck with it.

As I drove away from Pennhurst, mixed feelings filled my head. Working in Mayflower had been quite an adventure. I had touched on something mysterious and yet fascinating. One thing was for certain, I would never forget it.

Figure 6. Little girl is wispy, standing in the bottom, center

Figure 7. Half of boy's body

Conclusion

FOR DAYS AFTERWARD, the photo of the boy and the little girl ghosts lingered in my thoughts. I had shown the photo to family members to get their thoughts on the images. Perhaps I was hoping for an explanation. But everyone was shocked. Some had trouble seeing the little girl or making out her form. But the boy can easily be seen – especially on my daughter's phone, where she can enlarge it. The photographs are real. The boy was real and so was the small girl. Why they allowed themselves to be photographed on my final night at Pennhurst, I haven't a clue. Had I seen them sooner during the season, I might have quit in fear as others had done.

So who are the ghosts of Pennhurst? I'm not sure. I have a lot of ideas. But I won't go into speculation. In many ways working in the Mayflower increased my faith in God. After all, he is a spirit too. People are fascinated with the spirit world. This can be a dangerous attraction. Doors might be opened that cannot be closed. But the lure is there.

All of my life, the spirit world has been around me. I am always conscience of it but have learned to put up mental and spiritual blocks to protect myself.

My purpose of this book was to entertain, perhaps

enlighten in some ways. I have friends and family members who will never go to the Pennhurst haunt. It scares them just thinking about it. But they are curious and eager to read this book.

In conclusion, I want to say working in Mayflower was a fascinating experience. I got so much more than I bargained for when I took this Pennhurst job.

So is Mayflower really haunted?

Please. Don't take my word for it. Go and see for yourself.

But before you do, make sure your immunizations are up to date or you might just get the dreaded shot.

Hope to see you there!

CPSIA information can be obtained at www.ICGtesting.com
Printed in the USA
LVOW120502010313

322217LV00001B/188/P